S0-DMQ-844

FACULTY DEVELOPMENT THROUGH WORKSHOPS

FACULTY DEVELOPMENT THROUGH WORKSHOPS

By

CAROLE J. BLAND, Ph.D.

Associate Professor
University of Minnesota Medical School
Minneapolis, Minnesota

For

The Society of Teachers of Family Medicine

St. Philip's College Library

Foreword by

Theodore J. Phillips, M.D.

Professor of Family Medicine
University of Washington
Seattle, Washington

CHARLES C THOMAS • PUBLISHER
Springfield • Illinois • U.S.A.

Published and Distributed Throughout the World by
CHARLES C THOMAS • PUBLISHER
Bannerstone House
301-327 East Lawrence Avenue, Springfield, Illinois, U.S.A.

This book is protected by copyright. No part of it
may be reproduced in any manner without written
permission from the publisher.

© *1980, by* CHARLES C THOMAS • PUBLISHER

ISBN 0-398-03940-2 (Cloth)

ISBN 0-398-04002-8 (Paper)

Library of Congress Catalog Card Number: 79-9074

610.7
B642f

Library of Congress in Publication Data

Bland, Carole J
    Faculty development through workshops.

    Bibliography: p. 203
    Includes index.
    1. Family medicine — Teacher training.   2. Family medicine — Study and
teaching — Congresses.   3. Teachers' workshops.   I. Society of Teachers
of Family Medicine.   II. Title.
R833.5.B55   610'.7   79-9074
ISBN 0-398-03940-2

*With THOMAS BOOKS careful attention is given to all details of manufacturing
and design. It is the Publisher's desire to present books that are satisfactory as to
their physical qualities and artistic possibilities and appropriate for their particular
use. THOMAS BOOKS will be true to those laws of quality that assure a good
name and good will.*

Printed in the United States of America
WM-6

FOREWORD

The short-term workshop is one strategy commonly used for refreshing and extending faculty skills. While the method is popular with participants, planning and conducting such a workshop present a formidable challenge to the person responsible for its success. This book was clearly written with the needs of that workshop coordinator in mind. Dr. Bland's purpose is twofold: (1) to describe a process in enough detail to guide decision-makers without insisting they become experts in each area covered and (2) to support the process as outlined by references to the literature. These aims have been accomplished. Dr. Bland offers specific rules of thumb and timetables. She reports concensus recommendations gleaned from a thorough review of the literature. To the findings of this review, she adds insights gained through her own experience as a workshop coordinator and as a participant in the workshop study conducted by the Society of Teachers of Family Medicine in 1977. Thus this book is at once a how-to-do-it manual and a scholarly new contribution to the literature on faculty development.

The growth of family medicine demonstrates the need for faculty development and the use of workshops in addressing this need. In the 1960s, consumers and physicians were dissatisfied with limited access to medical care. Further, with increased specialization in medicine, patients perceived a loss of the personal attention they had known and appreciated in an era dominated by the general family doctor. These feelings produced support for a new effort to train family physicians in the United States. The resulting educational programs are based on several beliefs: (1) family physicians can provide high quality general care, (2) they are in a unique position to study systematically the problems encountered in pri-

7C421

mary care, and (3) they can produce new knowledge, skills, and understanding with which to approach that care. In short, current efforts in the education of family physicians assume that *family practice* as a medical specialty is based on *family medicine,* a clinical discipline. Consistent with that philosophy the first department of family medicine in a United States medical school was created in 1966. At about the same time, the first of the family practice residency training programs began. The American Board of Family Practice was formally accepted as the twentieth certifying board in the United States in February 1969. One decade later there are more than 100 medical school departments or divisions of family medicine in United States medical schools and 360 approved residency training programs.

This rapid development of a new clinical discipline created an intense need for faculty in the field. There was, and is, a need for family physicians and others to gain skills as teachers, educators, administrators, and scholars. There were, and are, great expectations of excellence in these academic efforts. Physicians serving as teachers in these programs are quite familiar with short (one day to one week) workshops as a means of updating and improving clinical knowledge and skills. Therefore, it was natural that they would be attracted to the workshop format for acquiring skills needed in their new roles as faculty. The American Academy of Family Physicians and the Society of Teachers of Family Medicine held regular meetings for faculty that allowed sharing of experience and ideas. These were crucial in the formation of standardized training programs and in the development of new faculty members. However, it soon became apparent that sharing experiences was not enough. There was a need for a more systematic way to improve academic skills.

Leaders of other disciplines had grappled previously with the question of how to promote faculty development. A body of experience and knowledge already existed, particularly in the educational literature. It remained for those working in family medicine to avail themselves of this knowledge and apply it to the family medicine situation. At this point the Society sought funding to conduct the pilot workshops mentioned above. This action resulted in a fruitful collaboration between the Society and Dr. Bland. The workshop study built on the findings of others, which had been collected and summarized by Dr. Bland. The results of the study affirmed the transferability of faculty development findings in other fields to family medicine and produced additional insights. This book presents the principles drawn from the field of faculty development and illustrates their use with examples from family medicine as well as other areas.

The Society of Teachers of Family Medicine is grateful to Dr. Bland for her efforts. On behalf of the membership I welcome this opportunity to express our thanks to her and to the Department of Family Practice and Community Health at the University of Minnesota, which supported her in this effort. Dr. Bland has acknowledged herein the efforts of her fellow members of the STFM planning committee that developed the workshop study and the individuals at the four institutions who conducted workshops for the Society. I add here the appreciation of the Society for their contributions. Finally, the Society of Teachers of Family Medicine appreciates the support of the Department of Health, Education, and Welfare (contract #231-76-0018) that made possible the 1977 workshops and the Exxon Foundation for its grant toward publication of this book.

Theodore J. Phillips, M.D.
President, 1978-79
Society of Teachers
  of Family Medicine

St. Philip's College Library

ACKNOWLEDGEMENTS

This book draws from many sources. The written sources are simple to acknowledge, via the references and selected bibliography. It is more difficult, however, to note in the text those persons who have had an important influence on me, and this book, through serving together on committees, speaking at length about faculty development, or critiquing my writings.

Thus, I wish to acknowledge here my gratitude to the members of the Planning Committee of the Society of Teachers of Family Medicine (STFM). This group directed a study with two goals: (1) to assess the effectiveness of the workshop format for promoting faculty development and (2) to determine guidelines for such workshops. This study was funded under DHEW Contract No. 231-76-0018. My involvement with this committee prompted me to intensify my investigation of the topic of faculty development and, ultimately, to write this book. The STFM Planning Committee included the following persons:

Edward Shahady, M.D., Project Director
Chapel Hill, North Carolina

John Arradondo, M.D., M.P.H.
Nashville, Tennessee

Richard Baker, M.D.
Chapel Hill, North Carolina

Carole Bland, Ph.D.
Minneapolis, Minnesota

Gerald Gehringer, M.D.
New Orleans, Louisiana

Magdalena Miranda, Project Officer
Department of Health, Education, and Welfare
Washington, D.C.

Leonard Masters, M.D.
Des Moines, Iowa

Patricia Plhak, Project Administrator
STFM Executive Director, 1975-1978
Lee's Summit, Missouri

As part of the study, prototypical faculty development workshops were developed and conducted during 1977 by the following:

Department of Family Practice, University of Iowa

Department of Family Practice, Michigan State University

Duke-Watts Family Medicine Program, Duke University

Psychology and Consulting Associates of San Diego and University Associates Inc. of San Diego in conjunction with Division of Family Medicine, University of California, San Diego

Wayne Welch, Ph.D., of the University of Minnesota and Robert Reineke, Ph.D., of the Search Institute in Minneapolis provided the committee with evaluation information.

In addition to the committee members listed, numerous staff and consultants for the participating institutions, and readers of early drafts of this book, several others must be mentioned. Patricia Plhak of the Minnesota Association for Children with Learning Disabilities, Deborah Spencer of the University of North Carolina, and Maureen Moo-Dodge of the University of Minnesota contributed significantly to the chapter on budget. This guidebook became a reality through the creative, thoughtful editing of Pamela LaVigne and the careful, accurate typing of Jacky Hanson.

I also wish to express my thanks to the Exxon Foundation, the Society of Teachers of Family Medicine, and the Department of Family Practice and Community Health at the University of Minnesota for their support of this book.

Parts of this book appeared in an earlier form in "Guidelines For Planning Faculty Development Workshops" by Carole J. Bland, *Journal of Family Practice* 5:235-241, August 1977.

C.J.B.

CONTENTS

FACULTY
DEVELOPMENT
THROUGH WORKSHOPS

Chapter 1

PURPOSE AND ORGANIZATION OF THIS BOOK

IMPETUS AND SCOPE

A very specific question was the stimulus for this book: How can family medicine faculty, whether physicians or professionals in other clinical or academic disciplines, be helped to function comfortably and efficiently in their roles as teachers, administrators, and scholar/researchers? Workshops were found to be an effective means of promoting faculty development and meshed well with the time constraints of family medicine faculty.

The research that lead to selection of the workshop format and to the development of guidelines for a successful workshop pointed up two important generalizations:

- Guidelines useful for faculty development workshops in family medicine are equally valid for faculty development workshops in other fields.
- These guidelines are essentially the same, whether for four hour, two day, or two week workshops.

Thus, although this book was prompted by an inquiry into two-four day faculty development workshops in family medicine, its recommendations are far from limited to that field or to workshops of that length only.

AUDIENCE AND PURPOSE

This guidebook was prepared primarily for the individual who has the role of workshop coordinator and the tasks of planning, conducting, and evaluating a faculty development workshop. The book provides essential workshop guidelines, explains their importance, and describes the sequence in which to commence the organizational steps. Others, such as department chairpersons or professional faculty developers, will also find this guidebook useful as a quick reference to and summary of relevant decisions and activities surrounding a faculty development workshop.

By synthesizing much of what has already been written about

3

workshops for faculty development then, this book provides a double service: (1) it is a reference to the literature on this topic and (2) it translates research findings into practical guides for those who plan and conduct workshops.

The following chapters may well serve another purpose also. Having marshalled the evidence presently available about workshops as a learning method, it is easy to see where gaps in knowledge exist. Perhaps this guidebook will become a springboard for further research, insight, and innovation in faculty development through workshops.

ORGANIZATION

Here is how the book is organized: The first chapters in the book provide an overview of faculty development through workshops. This chapter orients you to the rest of the book and tells how to put the information to best use. Chapter 2 outlines the need for faculty development and summarizes research supporting the two-four day residential workshop as an effective and appropriate means for facilitating the development of family practice faculty as well as faculty in other disciplines. Chapter 3, the Activities Checklist, is a chronological list of decisions a workshop planner must make, many of which must be completed long before the actual date of the planned workshop. If one of the activities is further discussed, the chapter reference is indicated.

Chapters 4 through 11 form the heart of the book, the "how-to" chapters. Each of the "how-to" chapters contains two sections: (1) rules of thumb — lists of recommendations for quality workshops — and (2) supporting evidence — a defense and discussion of the rules of thumb. The rules of thumb are a distillation of experience and pointers from many authors for assuring a quality workshop. Since each workshop is unique, the supporting evidence section discusses each recommendation so that you'll know how to adapt the rules of thumb for your particular situation. This discussion reviews briefly the relevant theory and research, with emphasis on the results of workshops in family medicine, and includes anecdotes and examples related to each recommendation.

The "how-to" chapters are organized to be conceptually consistent. Thus, they do not reflect the chronological order of the checklist. For example, the checklist frequently refers to the workshop objectives, from initial planning to final assessment. The topic of objectives is addressed once, however, in Chapter 8.

Here is how it is suggested you proceed. If you are unsure of just what faculty development is or unconvinced of the effectiveness of the workshop format, first read Chapter 2. If these concepts are familiar, read through Chapter 3, then skim the explanatory chapters.

After this initial dry run, stop. Taking the Activities Checklist as a master list, compare your workshop organization to it. Identify what decisions remain to be made, what commitments must be secured, and how long all of this will take. Clear-eyed realism is essential at this point to avoid a sense of being in over your head later. Can you document a need for your proposed workshop? Do you honestly have enough time and resources—both financial and personal—to carry off the proposal?

If you answer "no" to any of these questions, adjust your proposal accordingly—now. For example, if you have been asked to mount a workshop in two months but the preworkshop activities would take three months to complete, something has got to give. Or, perhaps you need two full-time individuals as workshop instructors, but you only have funds for one. Whether it's number of participants, objectives, or teaching strategies—somehow, the scope of the workshop must be reconsidered and possibly pared down.

If you answer "yes," then forge ahead. Use the Activities Checklist as a road map to your destination: a well-organized, smoothly run workshop that will produce the desired changes in participants. As necessary, return to Chapters 4 through 11 for background to many of the checklist items. If you can't find the fine point you're looking for in these chapters, or if you would simply like to do more reading in some areas, the references and bibliography will point you to other helpful printed sources. The list of faculty development consultants in Appendix XIV identifies persons you could contact directly regarding problems.

Chapter 2

FACULTY DEVELOPMENT: NEED, RESPONSE, STFM STUDY

College teaching is probably the only profession in the world for which no specific training is required. The profession of scholarship is rich in prerequisites for entry, but not that of instruction (1, p. xvii).

NEED FOR FACULTY DEVELOPMENT

Faculty development is a need among college faculty of all disciplines. This section describes the broad need for faculty development, the two-four day residential workshop as a means for meeting this need, and the response of one discipline, family medicine, to that need.

In articles and books, through university departments, national centers and professional organizations, the process and goals of faculty development are receiving much attention. Faculty development has been defined as a "process which seeks to modify the attitudes, skills, and behavior of faculty members toward greater competence and effectiveness in meeting student needs, their own needs, and the needs of the institution" (2, p. 720). Mechanisms such as attendance at professional conventions and conferences, recognition and monetary reward for publishing, sabbatical leave, and "moving up" by taking a position at another institution have traditionally kept faculty members up-to-date and stimulated in their field. While these efforts motivated faculty to develop as researchers and scholars, they did not necessarily encourage or reward those who wished to improve their teaching skills.

Other complicating factors came into play in the last fifteen years. Declining university enrollments in the late sixties virtually froze most faculty mobility. Without the continual influx of new faculty members, fewer changes were prompted from within academic institutions and the status quo seemed more and more to prevail. When calls for accountability and demands for instructor

7

evaluation were heard, a problem long acknowledged but rarely acted on was highlighted: Collegiate-level faculty are sorely untrained for the teaching and administrative tasks they must perform. Gaff names specifically what is lacking in their training: "Our colleges and universities are now staffed by faculty who, in general, have never studied the history of their profession, are unfamiliar with the topography of the educational landscape, are unaware of the professional literature in higher education, and have never been expected to formulate systematically their own philosophies of education or their views about teaching and learning" (3, p. 16).

While teachers in all disciplines face the problem of being inadequately prepared for their faculty responsibilities, this problem is particularly pressing for family practice faculty, most of whom are physicians. Like their colleagues in other fields, they share the need for training in teaching and administration. Unlike their nonphysician colleagues, they have generally not had an opportunity to acquire research skills. Thus, they have the additional deficit of little or no training in academic research.

Other characteristics of family medicine education increase the need for highly effective faculty members, such as the following:

- Because of the rapid growth of family medicine, there is a shortage of faculty.
- Many fields are integrated in family medicine faculty resulting in a highly diverse group.*
- As a relatively new discipline, most faculty members are former practicing family physicians, unfamiliar with academia.

RESPONSE TO NEED FOR FACULTY DEVELOPMENT: TWO TO FOUR DAY WORKSHOPS

The search for an effective means to meet the faculty development needs of family medicine faculty revealed that workshops are a frequently used and effective method of promoting faculty development in general (5). First, faculty development workshops have had significant long-term effects on faculty members' behavior.

---

*Rogers and Shoemaker describe such groups as heterophilus and find, typically, that highly heterophilus groups have communications and interrelation difficulties (4).

Second, the two-four day workshop suitably fits many faculty members' needs and constraints such as: scattered locations, limited time, and multiple needs — knowledge, skills, and attitudes.

Higher education faculty development programs commonly include workshops. Centra, in a survey of 1,044 college faculty development coordinators, found that the formats used to increase faculty effectiveness and comfort fell in the categories of "(1) workshops, seminars, or similar presentations; (2) analysis or assessment of instructors by students, by colleagues, by use of videotape, or by other means; (3) activities that involved audiovisual aids, technology, or course development; and (4) institutionwide practices such as sabbaticals and annual teaching awards" (6, p. 51).

Even though workshops are used for faculty development in general, the research that documents the effectiveness of the workshop approach is predominantly found in the medical education literature (5, 7-15).

Effectiveness

Wergin, Mason, and Munson (7) reported success with a variety of faculty development workshops conducted predominantly with medical faculty. Donnelly, Ware, Wolkon, and Naftulin (8) evaluated six weekend seminars for continuing medical education covering a variety of subjects. They found that, in general, cognitive gains and attitudinal changes were significant, as measured by multiple choice and true/false questions and semantic differential items. In another study, Koen (10) described a series of workshops in faculty educational development at Wayne State University, School of Medicine. Participants reported an average goal achievement of 4.2 on a 5-point scale where a rating of 5 indicated complete achievement of the program's preset goals.

Nerup, Thomsen, and Vejlsgaard (9) examined three pilot programs developed for training medical school teachers. Of the forty-six participants, thirty-one were physicians and fifteen were chemists. There were fifteen instructors. These courses, which sought to give participants basic principles as opposed to teaching skills, were quite acceptable to all participants and not one participant would have preferred a practical teaching course. However, half the physicians felt they needed further instruction of a more practical nature. Participants rated the courses highly. Various elements such as organization and technical aids averaged 4.5 on a 5-point scale with 5 representing the highest rating. Most thought the courses should be longer, although they ran twelve to fifteen hours. Teacher evaluations showed that the instructors believed participants had acquired much of the content of the courses. They used tests or papers to assess participant progress.

A follow-up one to two years later showed that most participants had made changes in their teaching behavior as a result of the workshops. For instance, thirty-seven said they now prepare goal statements for their courses; thirty-eight changed the organization of their teaching; twenty-nine found they needed to take more time to plan for teaching. These findings offer specific examples of the general rule: Workshops as a means of faculty development have significant and long-term effects on learners.

Suitability

Given that workshops are an effective means of promoting faculty development, which kind of workshop is best for faculty members with the constraints described above? Bergquist and Phillips outline four types of workshops (16):
- long-term residential, five days to two weeks
- short-term residential, two to four days
- extended on-site, three to twelve hours
- brief on-site, one to two hours

The long-term residential workshop is most useful when the objectives of the workshop are facilitated by establishing significant relationships among participants and staff. This type of workshop is particularly appropriate for changing the attitudes or values of participants. However, since many faculty work in small programs with few staff, and since even in large programs faculty are over-extended, it is difficult for such faculty to attend a long-term residential workshop.

The short-term workshop (two–four days) is the conventional adult training program often found in business, management, and continuing education. It focuses on a more specific set of objectives than the long-term residential workshop. The short-term workshop is usually residential and enables some relationships and trust to develop.

The extended on-site workshop (three–twelve hours) is the most common type for faculty development. This can be a most supportive format since it enables faculty members to try new behaviors in their home setting while still having the support of the faculty development program.

The brief on-site workshop (one–two hours) is usually devoted to very specific objectives such as "how to develop a seminar evaluation" or "how to increase resident-preceptor interaction in the clinic." It seldom addresses affective objectives nor does it develop the interpersonal relationships among participants that the residential workshops do. Nonetheless, it can build on existing relationships or supplement other long-term faculty development activities. Further, both the brief and extended on-campus workshops are relatively inexpensive since they do not involve housing or travel costs.

Because of the multiple needs, time constraints, and varied locations of many faculty, a residential workshop of short duration (two–four days) seems most appropriate to facilitate faculty development of persons in this group. The format offers many of the advantages of the long-term residential workshop:

- facilitating development of limited interpersonal relationships among faculty and participants
- physically removing participants from competing home responsibilities
- providing an environment appropriate for all types of objectives
- providing sufficient time for concentrated learning while requiring an absence of only a few days

STFM STUDY

Recognizing the need for faculty development and aware of the suitability of short-term residential workshops for family practice instructors, the Society of Teachers of Family Medicine (STFM), in 1977, conducted a study to assess the effectiveness of workshops for promoting faculty development (11-14). Since many of the examples mentioned throughout this guidebook are drawn from the STFM study, a brief description follows of the typical participant and the main findings (14).

Typical Participant

The study included a total of 115 participants in four workshops. The typical participant was male, had an M.D. degree, and considered family medicine his specialty area. He was either a director or codirector of a family medicine residency program in a community hospital. He had about two years' experience as a faculty member and had not previously attended a faculty development workshop (14).

Main Findings

During the first workshop session of each workshop, participants were asked to complete a Faculty Activities Rating Scale (FAR). (See Appendix X for a copy of the FAR.) The FAR listed the teaching, administrative, and academic abilities found in the original request for proposals. The FAR somewhat indirectly measured achievement in these abilities as a result of attending the workshops by asking participants for their perceptions of their knowledge of each ability. At the last session of each workshop and nine months after the workshop, participants again completed the FAR.

Comparing preworkshop and postworkshop FAR results shows that the workshops, viewed individually and collectively, were successful in significantly increasing participants' abilities to perform faculty functions (14). Participants left the workshop reporting that they were more knowledgeable about certain faculty abilities considered valuable for conducting family medicine training programs. In fact, the degree of change they recorded between before-workshop and after-workshop perceptions of their knowledge was much greater than what usually occurs in educational settings.

Comparison of preworkshop FAR and nine-month follow-up FAR results shows participants felt, even nine months later, that as a result of attending a faculty development workshop, they were significantly more knowledgeable in most of the faculty areas addressed by the workshops (14).*

---

*Just how close *perceptions* of knowledge gained come to judging *actual* knowledge gained is not well established. It seems reasonable to assume that there is a positive relationship between them. Strictly speaking, the before and after differences on the FAR show statistically significant gains in *perception* of knowledge. There are no statistics about actual changes in knowledge from the workshops.

Summary

There is a need for faculty development among all higher education faculty. Research shows that, in addition to its wide use, the two-four day residential workshop is one effective format for meeting this need. Workshops, convenient for many faculty, can facilitate enduring perceived change in participants' teaching, research, and administrative abilities. The rest of this book will guide you through the multistep components of organizing your own successful faculty development workshop.

Chapter 3

ACTIVITIES CHECKLIST

You don't have to turn the pages to find out: there are 105 numbered items on this list. Even with that number, it's not meant to include every detail you'll have to attend to when organizing your workshop. This Activities Checklist does outline all the fundamentals, however, and spells out many of the little points to look into as you proceed. It's arranged in approximate chronological order, approximate because the activities listed often go on concurrently and must be repeated as negotiations are conducted and decisions made.

The checklist is flanked by two columns. If one of the activities relates to a discussion elsewhere in this guidebook, the appropriate chapter reference is noted at the right. To the left is space for you to write the date by which you want to accomplish each activity.

How much time you'll need depends on the depth of the content, the size of the group, and other variables. Nevertheless, even under the most favorable conditions—say you're repeating what is basically a packaged workshop—you'll need at least three months to complete all the preworkshop tasks.

This checklist includes items adapted from the following sources:
- *How to Organize a Short-Term Education Workshop* (17)
- *Workshop Planning: A guide to considering, designing and planning educational workshops* (18)
- 50 Steps to a Successful Conference (19)

The main steps in planning and conducting workshops are listed below; the details of each are noted in the checklist.

Preplanning
  Specifying Needs and Seeking Funds
    Establishing the Basic Framework
      Selecting Participants and Finalizing Schedule
        Keeping in Touch
          Wrapping Up Preworkshop Details
          On Site
          After the Workshop

WORKSHOP ACTIVITIES CHECKLIST

Completion Date	Goals and Activities	See Chapter

Preplanning: The Gleam in Your Eye

_____ 1. Choose workshop coordinator and committee members 4

_____ 2. State tentative purpose of workshop 5

_____ 3. Describe likely participants 7

_____ 4. Identify possible sponsors 6

_____ 5. Identify potential funding sources 6

_____ 6. Define staff structure and assign tasks........................ 4

_____ 7. Draw up a rough budget....................................... 6

_____ 8. Secure approval from sponsors of these preliminary, general ideas 6

Specifying Needs and Seeking Funds: Reality Testing

_____ 9. Determine needs of potential participants...................... 5

_____ 10. Define criteria for accepting participants 5,7

_____ 11. Establish tentative goals and objectives........................ 5,8

_____ 12. Select tentative teaching strategies and related teaching materials 9

_____ 13. Estimate costs (consultants, site, equipment, etc.) 6

_____ 14. Figure tuition 6

_____ 15. Find a funding source... 6

_____ 16. Establish actual program budget 6

_____ 17. Obtain approval in writing of final budget...................... 6

The success of a workshop will depend largely on the way it is planned and on the arrangements made BEFORE the opening session (17, p.5).

Establishing the Basic Framework

Choose Dates and Site

_____ 18. Check tentative dates to be sure they don't conflict with dates of other conferences participants are likely to attend, holidays, high vacation periods, etc.

_____ 19. Determine final dates.

_____ 20. Contact possible sites by phone, screening them according to their responses to basic workshop requirements such as:

WORKSHOP ACTIVITIES CHECKLIST

Completion Date	*Goals and Activities*	*See Chapter*

a. Dates

b. Conference rooms, capacity, facilities for audiovisual materials

c. Guest accommodations

d. Dining facilities

e. Cost

_____ 21. Make site visits, collecting details on the following: 11

    a. Large conference room: capacity, location, can it be partitioned

    b. Smaller meeting rooms: capacity, location

    c. Controls for light, noise, and heat in meeting rooms

    d. Audiovisual equipment: available on site, site will arrange, usable in which rooms

    e. Guest rooms: number and type, distance from meeting rooms

    f. Hospitality rooms: capacity, location, furniture arrangement. Bar: cost, bartender provided. Bar charges: per drink, bottle, or case; paid by customers? if yes, via cash or coupon

    g. Registration and information area

    h. Meals: adequate seating, menu choices including beverages and snacks for coffee breaks, appetizers for receptions, minimum-maximum guarantee policy

    i. Transportation to and from airport and other arrival points

    j. Parking

    k. Recreational possibilities on-site and nearby (tennis, swimming, golf, shopping, tours)

    l. Cost

_____ 22. Notify officials of sites visited but not selected and thank them for their assistance.

_____ 23. Notify official of site selected 11

_____ 24. Send letter of agreement to site selected, specifying workshop requirements for each item under 21. above. In addition, be sure to:.. 6,11

    a. Advise staff to bill participants at their business address unless they request otherwise.

    b. State dates, times, places, and menu for all meals.

    c. For receptions, give protocol for head table and dress. Also request table decorations and flowers for honored guests.

_____ 25. Prepare master list of meeting and hospitality rooms that itemizes specific room characteristics. Send to site officials and planning committee members.

WORKSHOP ACTIVITIES CHECKLIST

Completion Date	*Goals and Activities*	*See Chapter*
_____	26. Contact Chamber of Commerce and convention/ tourism bureau for information and publicity pictures about local area...........	7
_____	27. If recreational activities require staff participation, assign staff ..	4

Choose Objectives, Teaching Strategies, Instructors, Materials, and Evaluation Methods

_____	28. Finalize objectives and select teaching strategies	8,9
_____	29. Contact potential workshop faculty. Involve them in detailed discussion of teaching strategies.............................	4
_____	30. Identify existing instructional plans that might be used..........	9
_____	31. Distinguish between those which can be used as is and those that need modification.......................................	9
_____	32. Develop modifications..	9
_____	33. Prepare new instructional plans for areas not covered above	9
_____	34. Develop evaluation instruments for each plan and for the entire workshop to ensure that goals are being met..................	10
_____	35. Plan one or two group social activities during workshop— reception, barbeque, etc.....................................	7

Draw Up Master Plan

_____	36. Prepare final copy for each instructional plan based upon objectives for each session	9
_____	37. Plan sequence of each session within the workshop............	9
_____	38. Allot time for each session	9
_____	39. Name instructors, speakers, or consultants who will conduct each session..	4,9
_____	40. Decide how many participant work groups will be formed. Relate selection of groups to total number of participants, characteristics of participants, optimum number of people in each group	9
_____	41. Distribute master plan containing all above details to all planning committee members	9
_____	42. Discuss master plan at preworkshop meeting	9
_____	43. Modify if needed	9
_____	44. Get written commitments from consultants, instructors, and speakers	4
_____	45. Confirm in writing also that consultants and speakers will present what you have asked them to present, as directed by the objectives	4
_____	46. Apply to appropriate agency for continuing education credits.	

WORKSHOP ACTIVITIES CHECKLIST

Completion Date	*Goals and Activities*	*See Chapter*

_____ 47. Establish procedures for recording all income received and expenses incurred 6

—

Prepare Announcements

_____ 48. Decide what type(s) of announcements to use (letter, brochure, booklet).

_____ 49. Include in announcement the following information: 5,7
- a. Workshop dates, location, accommodations
- b. Cost
- c. Clearly stated objectives
- d. Teaching strategies
- e. Continuing education credits (if applicable)
- f. Qualifications or prerequisites for admission
- g. Preworkshop activities
- h. Names of faculty
- i. Sponsor(s) and funding agency(ies)
- j. Special events
- k. Spouses and family invited or not
- l. Arrangements for spouses and families

_____ 50. Design announcement.

_____ 51. Prepare copy.

_____ 52. Get printing quotations.

_____ 53. Send final copy to graphic designer.

_____ 54. Approve layout and copy for printing.

_____ 55. Print announcements.

_____ 56. Send first press release.

Selecting Participants and Finalizing Schedule

_____ 57. Select participants from those applying 5,7

_____ 58. Inform applicants that they were selected or not selected 7

_____ 59. Affirm that final objectives of workshop meet needs of incoming participants 5,8,10

_____ 60. Send participants preworkshop teaching materials.

_____ 61. Prepare workshop agenda including a schedule of workshop activities, identifying the faculty and individual groups for each . . 9

Keeping In Touch

_____ 62. Contact site officials four to six weeks before workshop to review agreements 6,11

Faculty Development Through Workshops

WORKSHOP ACTIVITIES CHECKLIST

Completion Date		Goals and Activities	See Chapter
_____	63.	Review workshop needs periodically with site officials	11
_____	64.	Contact faculty weekly	4
_____	65.	Advise faculty of final objectives.	8,9
_____	66.	Contact faculty again to reaffirm that their planned presentations do correlate with participants' needs and the final objectives of the workshop	9
_____	67.	Forward to consultants, speakers, and instructors the following materials:	
		a. Packet of registration materials	
		b. Master plan	
		c. Evaluation	
_____	68.	Send out second press release.	

Wrapping-Up Preworkshop Details

_____	69.	Name staff person(s) responsible for materials and audiovisual equipment	4
_____	70.	Determine materials needed for each session, considering:	

a.	Handouts	o.	Screen
b.	Flip chart	p.	Spare bulbs
c.	Easel	q.	Projector extension cords
d.	Newsprint	r.	Microphones
e.	Felt pens	s.	Videotape equipment
f.	Masking tape	t.	Television monitors
g.	Blackboard	u.	Films
h.	Overhead projector	v.	Slides
i.	Light pointer	w.	Paper pads for participants
j.	Opaque projector	x.	Pencils
k.	Blank transparencies	y.	Name tags
l.	Grease pencils	z.	Bulletin boards
m.	Slide projector	aa.	Thumbtacks
n.	Film projector	bb.	Kitchen timer

_____	71.	Prepare a master list of all required materials, amounts needed, where, and when.
_____	72.	Check with site officials to see if equipment operators are available on site.
_____	73.	Make separate lists of materials according to their source of availability:
		a. Already on hand
		b. Available on site
		c. Obtained elsewhere

WORKSHOP ACTIVITIES CHECKLIST

Completion Date	Goals and Activities	See Chapter

74. For materials under 73c. above, specify how they will be acquired:
    a. Borrowed at no cost
    b. Rented
    c. Purchased
    d. Bought by participants
    e. Specifically produced

75. For items borrowed at no cost:
    a. Contact person or agency holding items.
    b. Negotiate conditions under which item will be received, used, and returned.
    c. If necessary, borrow equipment operator also.

76. For items to be rented or purchased:
    a. Identify vendors and rental agencies.
    b. Consult catalogs to prepare purchase or rental list.
    c. If necessary, secure services of equipment operator also.
    d. Submit requisitions for equipment purchase or rental.

77. Make sure that there are operators for all equipment and that they know when and where their services are needed.

78. Schedule production of materials by staff and identify staff member in charge.

79. Classify materials for convenient dissemination and use, e.g. Monday morning stuff.

80. Find secure space to store materials before workshop as well as secure storage space on site.

81. As materials are received, check that they are in working order. Place in storage area.

82. Arrange to transport materials to workshop site.

83. Have these things printed:
    a. Workshop agenda
    b. Workshop materials
    c. Workshop evaluations

84. Arrange hotel accommodations for consultants.

85. Reaffirm with instructors, speakers, and consultants agreements about dates, place, honorarium, and any special travel arrangements, e.g. airport pick-up 4,6

86. Rehearse workshop 9

87. Write news release for postworkshop article.

88. Notify local press of workshop dates.

89. Transport materials and equipment to site.

Faculty Development Through Workshops

WORKSHOP ACTIVITIES CHECKLIST

Completion Date	Goals and Activities	See Chapter

On Site

_____ 90. Arrive on site one day in advance or early on the first day of the workshop.

_____ 91. Once again, check working order of all equipment.

_____ 92. With designated liaison from site staff:......................... 11

    a. Review each item in letter of agreement.

    b. Compare room reservations tally with list of participants.

    c. Go over room arrangements for workshop faculty and staff.

    d. Confirm arrival times of participants who must be met and transported to the workshop site.

    e. Review schedule of meeting rooms and leave a copy with site liaison.

    f. Go over times, places, and food chosen for coffee breaks, meals, and receptions.

    g. If meals and lodging are prepaid, establish limits on participants' charges, e.g. spouses included or not, bar bill, long-distance phone calls, etc.

    h. Find out on-site arrangements for banking, recreation, and getting messages to participants during the workshop.

    i. Confirm check-out time.

    j. Spot-check guest rooms.

    k. Check meeting rooms for necessary details.

    l. Check hospitality room for size, furniture, bar.

    m. Make sure seating is adequate for meals.

    n. Set up area for registration and information.

_____ 93. During workshop, keep site officials informed and refer all problems to designated liaison.

After the Workshop

_____ 94. Prepare final participant list.

_____ 95. Classify and package materials to be stored or returned.

_____ 96. Check working order of borrowed and rented equipment.

_____ 97. Return borrowed and rented materials.

_____ 98. Send letters of appreciation to agencies lending materials or equipment.

_____ 99. Send letters of appreciation to appropriate site officials 6

_____ 100. Submit materials for continuing education credit.

_____ 101. Send letter of thanks to: 6

    a. Planning committee members and staff

WORKSHOP ACTIVITIES CHECKLIST

Completion Date		Goals and Activities	See Chapter
	b.	Sponsors	
	c.	Funding agencies	
	d.	Faculty, and also include payment of expenses plus honoraria if not yet given	
_____	102.	Prepare a report for sponsors, funding agencies, and other appropriate audiences. Include the folowing:..................	6
	a.	Workshop description	
	b.	Results of the immediate evaluation of the workshop	
	c.	Statement of income and expense	
_____	103.	Start long-term evaluation.....................................	10
_____	104.	Collect data	10
_____	105.	Send final report to sponsoring agencies and other appropriate audiences	6

A workshop—
Don't think it will change nothing:
Don't believe it will change everything (17, p. 48)

Chapter 4

NAME COORDINATOR AND DETERMINE STAFF ORGANIZATION

RULES OF THUMB

• Appoint a single individual to be responsible for coordinating the workshop—set deadlines for, monitor, and review all planning activities.

• Select a planning committee.

• Make explicit the areas of responsibility and communication channels for leader, committee members, sponsors, and faculty.

• Develop a work plan and a timeline.

> Anticipate snags—build flexibility into the work plan.
>
> Schedule planning meetings that last long enough and are announced well in advance.

• Select a teaching faculty considering the following pointers:

> Plan on a ratio of one full-time equivalent teacher for every ten participants (this can vary with teaching strategy).
>
> Be certain that teachers can relate to participants.
>
> Insist that core teachers be available full-time during the workshop.
>
> Avoid introducing into a workshop a teacher who has not interacted with other teachers nor coordinated his/her role with theirs.
>
> Involve "outside" or guest experts as fully as possible in both the planning stages and the actual workshop.

• Select a highly credible person (in participants' perception) to present the faculty, thus increasing their credibility.

SUPPORTING EVIDENCE

Effective organization is the most critical factor for having a workshop that is a successful learning experience for participants and a satisfying teaching experience for faculty. *Organization* refers to personnel in the organization—a capable coordinator with no qualms about assuming the full responsibilities of leadership, tal-

25

ented and hardworking people on the planning committee. *Organization* also refers to a process — think ahead to the myriad details of arranging the workshop. As the Activities Checklist (Chapter 3) shows, much of the work of planning, conducting, and evaluating a workshop occurs long before the workshop takes place. All the groundwork, as well as the actual workshop presentation and follow-up, demand effective leadership, able faculty and staff, and, above all, thorough planning.

Speaking with the voice of experience and well-considered opinion, several authors cite the following as critical organizational components of an effective workshop: coordinator, planning committee, harmonious working relationships, and faculty (7, 20-23). Let's examine each component more closely.

COORDINATOR AND PLANNING COMMITTEE

Connell and others stress the importance of a single, identifiable leader (21). This rule of thumb is reiterated by Gale who states that "because of the complex nature of educational management, practical responsibility should, if possible, be given to one person only" (23, p. 88). (Gale includes workshops under the broad term *educational management*.) The coordinator needs the dynamism and inspirational power of a coach, the planning prowess of an experienced cook, and the attention to detail of a tax auditor. The seemingly limitless energy of a four-year-old would be a distinct advantage, too! A well-prepared, enthusiastic coordinator will set a fine example for the many people whose efforts are melded into the workshop.

Planning committee members are chosen in a variety of ways, such as appointed by a department head or higher level chief, self-volunteered, selected or hired by the coordinator, or recommended by a sponsor.* Regardless of how the group is formed, the planning committee should include, besides the coordinator, a secretary, a respresentative of the intended participants, and a spokesperson for

---

*The sponsor is the person or organization that approves of your workshop and offers its name as a show of support to be used in conjunction with the workshop. The funding agency is the person or organization tnat pays all or part of the workshop expenses or that provides other means of support, such as office space or personnel. Often the sponsor and funding agency are the same.

the sponsoring agency(ies). Frequently, a committee member represents more than one of these. Once faculty are chosen, they too must be directly involved in workshop planning. Even "outside" speakers and guest faculty should be involved as much as possible in shaping the workshop before it convenes. The coordinator should solicit ideas from all committee members, but a democratic approach to decision making about the workshop is not the most likely to succeed.

A highly respected, local leader in the participants' field is an important ally, both within the planning committee and to the workshop public. Early in the program this person should strongly endorse the workshop's purpose and also introduce faculty as individuals he/she supports. To reinforce this announcement, it is very important that this local leader be present and actively participate in the workshop. Initial suspicion of faculty can be rapidly dissolved if a credible local leader shows willingness to expose himself/herself to these individuals.

WORKING RELATIONSHIPS

While there is no substitute for competent committee members, competence can go unused because of poor communication and relationships within the committee. Connell and others stress the necessity of clear lines of responsibility among the faculty development planners (8,20,21,23). Coordinator, committee staff, and faculty need a clear understanding of the entire workshop program. We hear from Gale again: "Co-ordination of decisions is a crucial aspect of educational management, and a feedback system must develop to facilitate this" (23, p. 87).

What can you actually do to assure clear communications and good working relationships? No doubt you've already worked out a few techniques that have helped you in other settings. Be sure to apply every technique you know during this workshop planning—to keep in touch with committee members, faculty, participants; to run productive meetings; to remember good suggestions or questions on which to follow up.

Here's one technique you might try. Set up a giant pad of newsprint on an easel in the meeting room. Arm a committee member with a broadtipped felt marker and have him/her keep track of questions and decisions made, noting them on the pad in full view of the committee. When discussion is complete for that meeting, substitute a blotter-size calendar for the notepad and transfer tasks and person responsible onto this timeline. Thus, there will be verbal and written agreement on who will do what, plus the calendar emphasizes visually what responsibilities members have accepted and how their individual tasks interrelate. Using a calendar also helps planners see that a deadline such as "our next meeting," for instance, really means their task must be done a week or more *before* the next meeting if it involves such things as being typed or copied.

It is important for the coordinator to retain control of all workshop activities, carefully monitoring and assisting all faculty and staff. You may find it helpful to confirm instructors' and committee members' tasks through memos. Particularly if much time elapses between meetings and phone conversations, it is easy to forget or misrecall who was going to do what, by when. Be sure to confirm formally, in writing, any final agreements regarding responsibilities, time commitments, expense reimbursements, or honoraria with instructors, consultants, audiovisual assistants, etc.

Setting aside time to build a sense of team among staff and faculty may be necessary, particularly if the planned workshop will be loosely structured, that is, dependent upon faculty to lead many activities independently. More than normal cooperation is needed during the planning phase for such workshops. To avoid confounding the normal group definition process that participants will be going through at the workshop, faculty and staff should not be unfamiliar with one another or, worse, bring unresolved antagonisms or uncertainty into the workshop.

Team building can be achieved with certain fairly simple exercises. Some hour-long group exercises simulate common problems encountered in ad hoc work groups. In one exercise, for example, participants typically have limited information, are arbitrarily assigned roles (including one of obstructing the process), and they must complete a common task within a set time. Afterwards they discuss the very real confusion, delays, and mistakes that resulted when all did not fully participate. Another possibility: at its first meeting, the planning committee may decide to get better acquainted by taking an activity break together, outside the formal meeting room. For example, a midafternoon dip in the pool was relaxing and aided cohesion for one STFM workshop planning committee.

FACULTY

One of the first things you'll need to guess at is the number of faculty to employ for the workshop. Here are recommended numbers from Bergquist and Phillips. "A workshop which involves intensive skills training and consultation should usually provide one staff member per five participants. On the other hand, a workshop in which general skills training and discussion occurs may be effectively conducted with an eight- or even a twelve-to-one ratio. Theoretical material can be presented with a twenty-to-one ratio, whereas many small group exercises can be led with ratios as high as thirty- or even forty-to-one" (16, p. 242).

What should you look for when selecting workshop faculty? It is critical that faculty be able, well-informed educators who can present themselves well and perform credibly before the participants at the workshop. Connell has quite a bit to say on this point:

> The staff should include someone with competence in the educational content that will provide the specific focus for the programme (for example, instructional strategies or evaluation methodologies). This simple requirement, however, is often overlooked because teachers for the health professions are inclined to think of themselves as competent in educational content because they have taught, even though they have not engaged in any sustained study of the science of education. . . . [Further, the faculty should include] someone skilled in the process of facilitating active group learning and individualized learning. . . . [And,] the inclusion of an evaluation expert will surely assist staff members (21, p. 95).

A 1973 World Health Organization study also emphasizes that workshop faculty include those whose primary training is in education. It does, however, recommend that "individuals who conduct such programmes [should be] sufficiently familiar with the unique problems of health professions education to be able to address themselves to the issues directly and not merely use experience derived from elementary or secondary education" (24, p. 7).

It seems reasonable, of course, to match faculty background with participants' background. As Rogers and Shoemaker put it, "One of the obvious principles of human communication is that the transfer of ideas occurs most frequently between a source and a receiver who are alike, similar, homophilous" (4, p. 14). (*Homophilous* is the degree to which pairs of individuals are similar in certain attributes, such as beliefs, values, education, and social status.) Gregory and Hammar, after presenting a course on teaching skills to twenty-one medical faculty at the University of Rhodesia, noted the problem of a lack of common language between the educators teaching the workshop course and its physician participants (22). In spite of concerted efforts to minimize educational terminology, participants complained of too much educational jargon. In subsequent courses this problem was partially solved by providing participants with a glossary of terms. On the other hand, Nerup, Thomsen, and Vejlsgaard found in their study of three programs for training physicians and chemistry teachers that it mattered little if the teacher of the course had much in common with the participants as far as subject matter background (9). Nevertheless, it follows common sense to do your utmost to reduce jargon and frame rhetoric in language common to participants.

Core faculty should also be able to attend all planning meetings and every day of the workshop. Several authors (23), as well as the STFM study (11,12), attest to the importance of having principal faculty members present throughout the entire workshop. Guest faculty can offer unique skills not present in core faculty, as well as the influence of a "visiting fireman." However, data from the STFM workshops indicate that guest speakers or speakers who were not continuously involved in the workshop activities or at least present a majority of the time are viewed as "outsiders" by participants, thereby decreasing their effectiveness (11,12).

Beyond these criteria, faculty, at least taken as a group, should be versed in a variety of teaching techniques and be able to work with different types of learners. Wergin, Mason, and Munson, speaking from some painful experiences, point out that faculty need to establish credibility early on:

> It may be that education and teaching has either rightfully or mistakenly gained a poor reputation in that people see this as a discipline with little to offer. Or it may be that teaching being the discipline it is, is about the business of giving away its secrets and is unable to maintain the mystique of other professions such as medicine and law that somehow seem to command more respect. In any

case, particularly with physicians, it is important for the educational consultant to establish credibility before assuming a colleague role. . . . Further, if the consultant is not particularly sensitive to the needs and feedback coming from the participants [he or she] will be viewed as unresponsive. Therefore the consultants will need to have a broad range of consultant skills, ranging from group dynamics to expertise in test construction and be prepared to deliver (25).

The local leader/ally can do much to assist faculty in gaining credibility. If a guest speaker is used, it is necessary to take exceptional steps to assure the credibility of this guest and to apprise him or her of the participants' objectives and experiences thus far in the workshop. Simultaneously, the role of the guest must be made very clear to the participants.

In addition to instructor credibility, "good rapport" between faculty and participants has also been found to be important by some researchers (7,8,16). Some suggest setting aside outside time for establishing relationships. It is difficult to tell if a potential faculty member is going to appear credible to participants and be able to establish a rapport with them. More than once, widely recognized leaders in a field have seemed perfect for a workshop but, as it turned out, were so out of their element, they failed to "connect" with participants. If you are unsure of a potential faculty member's ability to relate to your participants, call someone who has seen him or her present to your type of participants or who has actually been a member of a similar workshop or class where your potential faculty member presented. Do not take a chance on an unknown quantity. The last thing you want is to reinforce any negative biases participants might have about the worth of presentations on education, administration, or research.

Clearly then, all one needs to do when selecting faculty is to identify individuals with formal sustained training in education and the topics to be presented, plus experience in the participants' field, who are versed in many interpersonal skills, teaching, and evaluation, who can work with a variety of learners, and who are able to quickly establish and emanate credibility!

Summary

As stated at the beginning of this chapter, *organization* in-

cludes both the personnel in the organization and the process necessary to ensure good working relationships among them. Both of
these facets of organization are critical to the effectiveness of your
workshop as well as to the pleasure you and your crew find in the
many hours of preworkshop activities. The next chapter, "Assess
Workshop Needs and Set Participant Goals," addresses one of the
first tasks of the coordinator and planning committee.

Chapter 5

ASSESS PARTICIPANT NEEDS AND SET WORKSHOP GOALS

RULES OF THUMB

• Identify the general areas of need of the workshop's target population, by relying solely on a needs assessment tailored to that group, or by using information produced by needs assessments from similar groups, or by doing both.
• Whichever approach is chosen, be sure that the needs assessment covers the following:

The intended participants' perceived needs
Participants' needs as others perceive them (e.g. department heads)
Likely needs of faculty as demonstrated by task analysis or identified by experts

• Base workshop goals on results of the needs assessment.
• Limit the number of goals to only those that are relevant and realistically attainable during the type and length of workshop planned.

SUPPORTING EVIDENCE

The preceding chapter discussed organization—name coordinator, assemble a planning committee, select faculty. If you recall the opening sections of the Activities Checklist, you'll remember that this group has a lot of guessing to do right away. A workshop for whom? To accomplish what? Costing how much? Answers to these questions must be roughed out in order to solicit support from funding sources and institutional sponsors.

This chapter describes the first task the planning committee must tackle for which a guess is never acceptable: conducting a needs assessment of the workshop's intended participants. Needs assessment, "the process by which one identifies needs and decides upon priorities among them" (26, p. 254), is the first step toward setting workshop goals and later, specific workshop objectives. A variety of sources are used to identify and rank needs, such as the participants themselves or lists of minimum competencies for faculty. Results of the needs assessment are the foundation you build on to determine what specific behaviors your workshop should and could best facilitate in faculty members.

No wind is favorable for a ship that knoweth not its destination.
Aristotle

NEEDS ASSESSMENT

As many investigators have shown, workshop goals must be relevant to participants' needs and realistically attainable through the workshop activities and time period (7,10,15,21,22,24). Although many variations exist, there are two basic models of needs assessment: the Competency Model Method and the Problem Analysis Method. Both offer ways of finding discrepancies between actual and desired ability; both offer, in other words, ways of finding where a need for change exists.

The Competency Model delineates the basic competencies required of a faculty member. In this model, needs are defined as those required competencies that participants lack or wish to improve. The Competency Model presupposes that you have a list of the essential abilities faculty members should ideally possess. You could draw up such a list in several ways:

- Search the literature for competencies required of collegiate-level faculty in general and in the field(s) of the intended participants in particular.
- Consult experts for their opinions.
- Conduct a task analysis.

Many articles outline the behaviors a faculty member needs to carry out the three major faculty roles of teacher, administrator, and scholar/researcher. (3,7,10,20-22,24,27,28).* The teacher role

---

*Clinician is a significant additional role of physician faculty. Providing community service is an additional responsibility of all university-based faculty, as well. Because these two roles are more appropriately addressed in other forms (such as the extensive network of continuing professional education), this handbook focuses on the three major roles named above.

involves such things as assessing the abilities of incoming students, planning instruction, using various teaching strategies, and preparing instructional materials (texts, films, modules). The administrator role encompasses activities from participating in faculty and committee meetings to preparing budgets and managing personnel. The scholar role includes activities such as regular reading in one's discipline, conducting research both in laboratory and real-life settings, and writing in one's field. Appendix I lists minimum abilities for each faculty role.

The Problem Analysis Method does not identify needs by locating discrepancies between competencies expected of faculty and their present abilities. Instead, this approach simply asks faculty to delineate areas in which they think they have a problem (29).

FOCUS OF YOUR NEEDS ASSESSMENT

While teaching is a primary activity of most faculty (and participants will probably rate it as one of their priority needs), teaching is by no means the only activity of faculty members. Other areas, such as research and administration, should not be ignored. In fact, Gaff cites Quehl who says that "a major shortcoming of this growing faculty development movement is that the programs created in its name tend to focus on the faculty member as a teacher (instructional development) while ignoring other faculty roles that are critical to the effective instruction: as persons (personal development) and as organizational members (organizational development)" (30, p. 28). Phillips reinforces this statement. "Any attempt at instructional change," he says, "that focuses merely on the role of the faculty member as an instructor and neglects the implications of instruction on his or her other roles can, at best, be only minimally successful" (28, p. 14). When planning a needs assessement, particular attention should be given to the faculty roles of scholar/researcher and administrator, as well as teacher.

Some researchers have pointed out that certain knowledge and abilities do not fit neatly into the three faculty roles, although college faculty need them all the same. For instance, it is often urged that teachers not only be able to perform "teacherly" skills, but they must also understand theories of learning and education (5,9,20,24). Fulop, writing about training teachers of health personnel for the World Health Organization, says teachers are "working in the dark" if they haven't studied educational psychology and don't understand the process of learning (31).

Connell and colleagues think the critical element missing in faculty development programs is instilling in faculty an inquiry approach or experimental mind-set toward their own educational responsibilities and practices. Her research over five years with 100 faculty members in health professions suggests that the development of an inquiry approach in faculty results in higher student ratings of their teachers' abilities and does, in fact, increase faculty behaviors that facilitate student thinking (32).

With some sense of the target population and on the basis of their own beliefs in these areas, planning committee members could decide that the needs assessment should address the items Fulop and Connell identified, in addition to those that pertain directly to faculty skills in the three basic areas.

NEEDS ASSESSMENT STRATEGIES

How exactly do you go about identifying participants' needs according to one of these models? Many strategies exist. Although they are often referred to as objective and subjective strategies, the distinction between them is somewhat blurred. Examples of objective strategies include simulation tests and critiques of performance using a standard rating scale. Self-rating of faculty behaviors is considered a subjective technique.

The STFM pilot workshops provide examples of both needs assessment models and objective and subjective techniques. Several pilot workshops used the Competency Model carried out with both subjective and objective assessment strategies. (Recall that the Competency Model is based on a list of minimal competencies that are thought to be essential.) For example, one planning committee prepared a list of required faculty abilities. Using this list as a yardstick they did the following:

- observed actual teaching on videotapes (objective)
- critiqued curriculum materials (objective)
- asked participants to choose from the required faculty abilities those in which they felt competent (subjective)

One workshop committee developed an exercise on objectives that could have served as a Competency Model approach to the needs assessment for their workshop. (A copy of the exercise is included in Appendix III.) The planning committee could have simply analyzed the responses participants gave to this exercise to discover what skills in writing objectives needed to be facilitated through the workshop.

Another workshop established its objectives entirely through a Problem Analysis approach called "Nominal Group Process." This method enabled group members, with the help of a trained group facilitator, to identify and establish priorities among their own self-perceived, work-related problems (33). Thus, through group process, a set of faculty development problems was identified and arranged according to consensus priority.

Some of the pilot workshops combined the Problem Analysis Model with the Competency Model and used both objective and subjective techniques. In one case, participants were asked to do the following:

- List problems they felt in performing effectively and comfortably as a faculty member (Problem Analysis, subjective). Later they were asked to rank these problems. (See Appendix II.)
- Rate their perceived level of performance for each faculty competency to be covered in the workshops (Competency, subjective). (See Appendix III.)
- Complete a test on objectives (Competency, objective). (See Appendix III.)
- Complete a simulation that the planning committee could compare to expected competencies (Competency, objective). (See Appendix IV.)
- Prepare a videotape that the planning committee could analyze for evidence of the required abilities (Competency, objective).

The workshop objectives could then be based on the areas of need identified using both models of needs assessment: (a) areas that learners felt were problems before referring to any competency list, and (b) the basic required competencies on which the learners were demonstrably poor performers as shown by the simulation, videotape, or self-report.

SOURCES TO ASK ABOUT NEEDS

In all of the examples above, information about the needs of participants was gathered from the participants, either through objective assessment or simply by asking them to identify the areas in which they believe they need further development. There are other sources from which you can collect information. You may want to ask people such as department heads, deans, or content experts in education, research, and academic administration to indicate from their perspective the most appropriate needs for your workshop to address. Their opinions may suggest that an area remain in the workshop in spite of low participant ranking. For instance, a department head may perceive a great need for increased administrative abilities among the faculty, whereas faculty members may perceive their administrative skills as already adequate.

If you cannot conduct a needs assessment specially designed for the intended audience of your workshop, you may find it helpful to examine the faculty needs assessments that others have performed. While at the Association of American Medical Colleges, Jason developed and administered simulation problems on basic teaching skills and concepts to a sample of medical school faculty across the nation (34). (See Appendix V for an example of one of the simulation problems used.) The results of this assessment through simulations were used to identify development needs of the individual faculty member and those needs common to many faculty members that might be addressed by national workshops, manuals, etc. Also, the American Association of Osteopathic Colleges, the Society of Teachers of Family Medicine, and the STFM workshops planning committees are groups who have conducted needs assessments from which planners of workshops for medical faculty could extrapolate in setting workshop goals.

SETTING GOALS

Remember:
* *Goals must be relevant to learners and accomplishable in your workshop.*
* *A workshop cannot meet everyone's needs.*

Once the needs of your learners are identified, select from among them only a few needs to be addressed by the workshop. Recently, the author ranked the needs to be addressed in a series of faculty development workshops through a survey that asked faculty members to rate their ability level in various faculty areas as well as the ability level they thought they should have. Those areas in which the greatest discrepancy existed between the ability level faculty members currently possessed and the level they thought they should have were addressed in subsequent workshops. (See Appendix VI).

So that you can concentrate on goals pertinent to participants, you may have to restrict enrollment according to criteria such as age, position, specialty, experience as faculty members, and percentage of professional time devoted to faculty commitments. For example, a high priority need for program directors or department heads may be how to prepare budgets or how to recruit teachers. While highly relevant to program directors, these needs are not likely to be areas of high interest or need for instructors or part-time clinical preceptors, nor for faculty members charged with undergraduate curriculum development.

Select goals that can be accomplished through your workshop. You simply may not have the faculty, money, time, or equipment to address some of the high priority needs of your potential participants. Certainly, you cannot meet all their needs in three or four days. It is a bit like deciding how to pay bills at the end of the month. Try to hit the most relevant and most urgent areas of need while pleasing as many participants as possible without promising more than you can deliver.

Don't forget to inform participants about the goals that have been established for the workshop. These goals must be stated in promotional materials. In addition, it is important to announce the goals and objectives on the first day of the workshop. If participants were surveyed about their perceived needs, you may wish to report their responses and how these were translated into the workshop's goals and objectives. This announcement helps to assure participants that their needs have been considered.

Summary

Even though, in the early stages of planning, the workshop is sketched in broad strokes, the picture must become more detailed by delineating goals and objectives. A needs assessment of the workshop's intended participants forms the data base for selecting your goals and objectives.

Chapter 6

PREPARE BUDGET

RULES OF THUMB

- Prepare a rough estimate of expenses likely to be associated with planning, conducting, and evaluating the workshop.
- Secure tentative approval of the workshop from the sponsor/funder, based on the preliminary estimates of expenses and income.
- Identify and contact potential funding sources.
- Carefully estimate all expenses and income associated with planning, conducting, and evaluating the workshop.
- Prepare actual program budget listing expense and income estimates.
- Adjust program budget, if necessary.
- Obtain written approval of the budget from the sponsor/funder.
- Keep accurate and detailed records of income received and expenses incurred; be consistent with the accounting requirements of your institution.
- Prepare periodic financial reports.
- Use periodic financial reports to make any necessary modifications in the workshop.
- Prepare and send a final report to the sponsor, funding agency, and other appropriate audiences.

SUPPORTING EVIDENCE

A budget is your financial blueprint. It is nothing more than an itemized summary of planned expenses and income for a given period. Usually it embodies as well a systematic plan for meeting expenses. If you carefully prepare a budget and use it throughout the workshop process, your financial specifications most likely will be met.

In the next pages you'll find simple guidelines for planning, preparing, monitoring, and concluding your workshop budget. They are guidelines not rules because financial systems vary from institution to institution and a fiscal requirement at one institution may be unnecessary at another.

BUDGET PLANNING

Although you don't need to reach for a calculator with your first thought about a workshop, you should quickly begin to think in financial terms. Will your institution or organization support your time and others' time to plan and conduct this workshop? Is it likely that foundations, governmental agencies, or other funding sources will financially support the program? Are there individuals who would spend time and money to participate in your workshop?

Obviously, "no" to all these questions will preclude further planning. Assuming, however, that human and financial resources are available to support the workshop, the first step is to plan a rough estimate of expenses likely to be associated with planning, conducting, and evaluating the workshop. These estimates are necessary to secure approval of the workshop from your sponsor, to obtain support from a funding source, and to keep you from getting into financial difficulty.

How do you arrive at a rough estimate? One way is to refer to the experience of others. Costs of previous instructional programs, when expressed as cost per participant per instructional hour, provide a base figure to use in making the first rough projections of your workshop expenses. Cost per participant hour is obtained by dividing the total program cost by the number of participants times instructional hours:

$$\frac{\text{Total Program Costs}}{\text{No. of Participants} \times \text{No. of Instructional Hours}}$$

The Society of Teachers of Family Medicine found that the average cost per participant instructional hour for workshops was $26.55 (11,12). The cost of other types of delivery systems has ranged from $4.80 to $20.80 per participant instructional hour (12).

To illustrate how cost per participant hour is used to derive a "ballpark" expense calculation, let's say you want to conduct a workshop similar to those sponsored by the Society. You anticipate there will be thirty participants at your workshop and that they will receive twenty-one hours of instruction. The cost per participant instructional hour times the number of hours times the number of participants equals total expense ($26.55 × 30 × 21 = $16,726.50).

One of the reasons for first preparing a rough estimate of expenses is that considerable lead time is necessary when dealing with foundations and other funding sources. (Securing funds from internal and external sources is discussed elsewhere in this chapter.) Before soliciting funds from any source, secure tentative approval of the workshop from your sponsor. This may save you from an embarrassing situation later on, such as being awarded a grant from a pharmaceutical company only to find that your university policy prohibits acceptance.

BUDGET PREPARATION

Included in the budget preparation process are the tasks of carefully estimating and listing all expenses and income, adjusting the program budget if necessary to meet your objectives, and, finally, obtaining approval of the budget.

Estimating Expenses

Collecting expense estimates is facilitated by grouping expenses into various categories. The categories can vary, of course, depending on the requirements of the workshop. The following are some common categories:

- Personnel — planners and teachers, secretaries and assistants, consultants and speakers
- Travel — transportation plus room and board for personnel and, if applicable, participants
- Facility — meeting rooms, food and refreshments, entertainment or special programs
- Administrative — supplies, equipment, telephones, graphics and reproduction, postage and freight

After establishing expense categories for your workshop, determine probable expenses in each category for all phases of workshop activities, from the first preplanning activity to the postworkshop details. The Activities Checklist (Chapter 3) will assist you in identifying potential costs. If an activity pertains to your workshop and has budgetary implications, estimate how much time and money will be needed.

When collecting expense information, be sure to obtain written cost estimates, in the form of bids or quotations, for any purchases, rentals, or services over a specified amount (usually $100, although this amount may vary). This is especially important when you are comparing various hotel facilities. Since rates can vary significantly, ask the sales and catering manager to provide written quotations for the following:

- various types of guest and meeting rooms (plus any additional costs for special seating arrangements, etc.)
- meals and refreshments, including gratuity, service charges, and tax
- audiovisual equipment and operator(s)
- any other special requirements for your workshop

Later, after selecting a facility, you will want to make sure these items are covered in an appropriately signed contract.

Unless you need a complete cost accounting for the workshop, you may not need to include the following in your estimates, as they often do not involve "out of pocket" expense:

- items you will borrow
- time faculty and staff will donate
- any other costs that will not be paid out of your budget

(These costs were included, however, in some of the cost per participant hour figures presented earlier, which accounts for the larger figures.) The sample budget sheet in Appendix VII provides a convenient format for expense estimates.

Estimating Income

Income from Tuition Sources

Workshop income is derived from participants' tuition and fees, plus financial support from foundations, governmental agencies, and the sponsoring institution. The most common sources of support are tuition and subvention from the sponsoring institution.

Estimating income from participants is simple. First, estimate what you will charge for workshop tuition, keeping in mind the going rate for similar workshops. Obviously, if several workshops are intended for the same participants, your tuition price must be competitive. On the other hand, if your workshop is the first to address, uniquely and innovatively, a high priority need for a large number of people, then price may be no object. Next, estimate any additional fees that you must collect, such as participants' lodging, meals, and transportation. To calculate total income from participants, multiply the sum of tuition plus fees by the total number of anticipated participants.

Income from Nontuition Sources

Estimating nontuition income includes identifying potential funding sources and presenting proposals to them.* Begin by taking a close look at the audience, purpose, and expenses for your workshop. How you define these parameters will suggest where you should turn for success in securing funds. When you eventually prepare a proposal and approach a potential funding agency, you will need to explain these and other aspects of your workshop in detail.

Nontuition funding sources are either internal or external. Internal funding sources are those located within institutions to which you also belong, such as college or university, corporation, hospital, or professional society. External sources have no affiliation with your institution. Examples include governmental agencies and foundations, such as the Department of Health, Education, and Welfare and the W.K. Kellogg Foundation.

Generally, internal sources are interested in funding projects that focus on their constituents, are short-term, and require smaller budgets. They often have predetermined funding priorities also. You can inquire about the possibility of internal funding from sources such as your own department, as well as the small grants program, center for educational development, or research and development division of your organization. Internal funding sources are usually preferable for your workshop for the following reasons:

- Awards can usually be made more quickly than by external sources.

---

*Recall that the sponsor is the person or organization that approves of your workshop and offers its name as a show of support to be used in conjunction with the workshop. The funding agency is the person or organization that pays all or part of the workshop expenses or that provides other means of support, such as office space or personnel. Often the sponsor and funding agency are the same.

- These sources are usually flexible, making it easier to negotiate budget items.
- Since you are located within the same institution from which you seek funds, personal channels can be used to your advantage.
- Justifying your budget to an internal source is likely to be easier because you share the same broad goals.

Compared to internal sources, external funding sources generally prefer projects of greater scope, for example, projects with regional or national impact or those developing model programs. External sources usually have predetermined funding priorities also, as well as extensive eligibility and information requirements for proposals. Predictably, external funds usually support projects with a longer timeline, three to five years, and larger budgets, $20,000 or more annually. Thus, soliciting external funds for short (two–four day) faculty development workshops may not be a viable alternative for the following reasons:

- It takes considerable time and effort to justify your needs and workshop plans to an outside agency with its own priorities.
- You lose time (months) while your proposal is considered.
- The cost of preparing the proposal may far exceed your resources.
- Your proposal will be compared to a large number of competitors, thus decreasing your chances of success.

Nevertheless, there are external funding sources and they do fund proposals. References that will help you identify potential external funding sources are listed below.

- *Catalog of Federal Domestic Assistance* (35). Lists grants, loans, scholarships, and technical assistance. Gives program objectives, eligibility requirements, telephone numbers for more information. Updated yearly.
- *Foundation Directory* (36). Lewis (ed). Lists, by state, about 2,500 foundations with minimum assets of $1,000,000 or that award $500,000 or more annually.
- *Annual Register of Grant Support* (37). Describes programs of governmental agencies, foundations, corporations, community trusts, unions, educational and professional associations, and special interest groups.

- Foundation directory for your state (if available). For example, *Minnesota Foundation Directory* (38) and *Illinois Foundation Directory* (39), both by Capriotti and Capriotti, are excellent resources for Minnesota and Illinois grant seekers.
- *Foundation News.* Section called "Foundation Grants Index Bimonthly" reports grant awards of $5,000 or more. Indices, plus annual reports, press releases, and other information, cumulated annually as yearbook, *The Foundation Grants Index* (40).

Requesting Funding

Regardless of which nontuition funding source you pursue, internal or external, it is very important that you prepare a clear statement of the major elements of your workshop before approaching a potential source. Of course, the format of your proposal will vary according to the requirements of the institution or agency. Also, its detail increases as you move from internal to national sources and from small budget to large budget requests. Nevertheless, any presentation should address at least the following:

RATIONALE: What problems or deficits exist that can be met by your workshop? How critical are these problems or needs? Why is your proposed workshop an effective way to meet the problem or need?

GOALS AND OBJECTIVES: Specifically, what abilities will participants achieve as a result of attending your workshop? How will achieving these goals help solve the problems or needs addressed under Rationale?

STRATEGIES: What methods will you use for accomplishing the stated goals and objectives of the workshop? Why are these the preferred strategies?

AUDIENCE: Who are to be the participants of your workshop? How will they be identified? How will these people, having achieved the workshop goals and objectives, help solve the problem or need addressed under Rationale?

PERSONNEL AND MATERIALS: What staff, facilities, and equipment will you use to facilitate the planning, conducting, and evaluating of your workshop? Why are these the preferred faculty, staff, facilities, and equipment?

EVALUATION: How does this evaluation ascertain if your workshop has helped solve the problems or needs addressed under Rationale? How do you know participants have achieved the objectives? What methods will you use to assess the cost-effectiveness of your workshop?

BUDGET: What expenses and income do you expect to result from your workshop? What is the source and justification of each expense and income?

There are several excellent, readable resources that will talk you through the steps of grantsmanship in more detail. Two such aids are *Grants: How to Find Out About Them and What to Do Next* (41) and "Program Planning and Proposal Writing" (42).

What happens *after* you submit your proposal to an external funding source is outlined in Appendix VIII. The same information for internal funding sources is not included since internal funding processes are usually unique to each institution and may operate under informal guidelines. For example, it may be as simple as a call to your department head or dean and a follow-up letter addressing the above areas. Approval or disapproval usually occurs within a few weeks. Or it may involve a formal application to the committee administering your university's small grants program.

CONSTRUCTING THE ACTUAL PROGRAM BUDGET

Once you have estimated all the probable expenses and income associated with your workshop, prepare the actual program budget by listing the estimates under the appropriate budget categories. Appendix VII provides a form for this purpose. Subtract total expense from total income to determine whether your workshop, without any adjustments, would have a net loss, break even, or have a net profit.

Unless your first program budget yields precisely the desired results—that is, your income equals your expenses or your income exceeds your expenses—you will need to adjust your program budget. Since one seldom hears complaints about a net profit, methods of increasing expenses and/or decreasing income will not be delineated here. By far, the more common situation after the first pass of the budget is a net loss. To correct this, you can increase income, or decrease expenses, or do both. To increase income, it may be possible to do the following:

- Attract and support more participants without adding to the cost or sacrificing the quality of the educational experience.
- Charge higher tuition and fees.
- Obtain additional support from funding sources or the sponsor.

To decrease expenses, it may be possible to do the following:

- Borrow more (staff time, AV equipment, etc.).
- Use less expensive materials and teaching strategies.
- Cut back the number of faculty.

Remember, if you make any adjustments, you must obtain written approval of the workshop modifications and the revised program budget from the sponsor and any other funding source.

BUDGET MONITORING

As mentioned above, bookkeeping policies and procedures vary from institution to institution, and frequently within institutions. A general rule of thumb calls for keeping accurate and detailed records of income received and expenses incurred, in complying with the specific requirements of the institution.

Periodic financial reports should be prepared in order to monitor the budget. It is suggested that you prepare them monthly. Although such reports may not be required by the funding institution, they are a valuable tool for the workshop planner in controlling income and expenditures as they occur. The workshop coordinator should use periodic financial reports to make any necessary modifications in workshop income and expenses. For example, if you note that tuition income is down from the budget, you may want to launch an additional promotional mailing to attract more participants. See Appendix IX for a sample financial report form.

CONCLUDING THE BUDGET

After the workshop is over, there are several budget-related details to which the workshop coordinator must attend. It is best to hand faculty their honoraria on the last day of the workshop. As soon as you know faculty members' expenses, send payment with a letter of thanks for their participation. A final report should be prepared and sent to the sponsor, the funding agency (along with a letter of thanks), and any other appropriate audiences. This report should include the following:

- description of the workshop
- results of the immediate evaluation
- final statement of income and expense

The statement of income and expense is similar to the periodic financial report (see Appendix IX). If you will be conducting a follow-up evaluation, you will need to amend your figures, plus send an amended report, after the long-term evaluation is complete.

Summary

Each step in the budget process is a means of summarizing at a point in time the status of the workshop's three key financial concerns: income, expense, and the difference between them. After estimates are made, actual dollar amounts must be determined. How much will you receive? What will your expenses be? Once monies are being exchanged, it is important to record and monitor all transactions. Last of all, an accounting of all financial activities should be included in the workshop's final report.

Chapter 7

SELECT AND KEEP IN TOUCH WITH PARTICIPANTS

RULES OF THUMB

- Select participants considering the following points:

    Match participants' needs with workshop goals.

    Cluster participants with similar faculty and workshop experience.

    Choose participants likely to be change agents (based on past performance, present position, training, expressed interest), that is, persons who can carry out the changes themselves or who can stimulate others to do so.

    Have two or more participants from the same program or department.

    Accept only volunteers.

    Allow no nonparticipant observers.

- Avoid a disproportionate number of participants from any single program or department, unless workshop is designed for only one program.
- Limit enrollment to a ratio of ten participants for each full-time workshop teacher (this can vary with teaching strategy).
- Limit total enrollment usually to thirty people.
- State explicitly the objectives and teaching strategies for the workshop in all publicity about it, especially if nontraditional content or procedures will be included.
- Set the tone—formal, casual—for the workshop in communications about it. Maintain that approach throughout all dealings with participants.
- Maintain timely contact with applicants and participants.
- Provide time during the workshop for informal interactions among faculty and participants.

SUPPORTING EVIDENCE

Every workshop needs and exists for the participants. Just who are they? What special qualities and characteristics should they have? Where should they come from? How do you contact them?

Most important, you should select participants whose needs are addressed by the objectives of the workshop (7,10,17,21,23,43). (See Chapter 5 for assessing needs of participants.) For example, a workshop designed to help beginning instructors develop exams will not meet the immediate needs of department heads or deans.

It is also important to consider participants' backgrounds as faculty members and as workshop attenders. New faculty, with little workshop experience, will likely need a different format than frequent workshop attenders (7,16). Wergin, Mason, and Munson identify two primary types of learners (7). The first type know little about teaching and are afraid to expose their teaching limitations. These are passive learners who prefer a lecture that will give them answers. This type of learner will benefit most from "advance organizers," things that let them know what is going to happen and that give them background information ahead of time, a full outline of the entire program, and readings to go through before it starts. The second type of learner is more advanced and will benefit from different instructional strategies. Discussion is particularly useful for this type of learner. So, it helps to cluster learners with similar faculty and workshop experience.

If possible, participants should hold positions of influence in their home environment so that they can implement their ideas and stimulate others (21). Certainly, their attendance at the workshop and subsequent work at home should be voluntary and have the official support of the department head and/or program director (21).

Connell recommends choosing at least two participants from the same institution so that upon returning home they will be able to support each other (21). However, STFM workshop planners found it necessary to balance this rule of thumb against problems arising from having a disproportionate number of participants from a single program (11,12). One of the STFM workshops had several faculty members from the same program who had an agenda of their own to work on. When they discovered the workshop had not allotted time for this, they decided to leave the workshop early to attend to their personal matter.

It's difficult to provide a rule of thumb for how many participants to have at a workshop. The optimal total will be influenced by virtually every workshop variable: type of objectives, participants' background, teaching strategies, monetary and space resources, and so on. In deciding on the number of participants for your workshop, you could be guided by Bergquist and Phillips's (16) suggestions about faculty-participant ratios cited in Chapter 4. Also, the STFM study found that a variety of teaching strategies were compatible with workshops of around thirty participants (11,12).

You should establish clear eligibility requirements to attract the type of applicants you want. These requirements, as well as complete program information (workshop objectives, faculty, preworkshop activities, teaching strategies, and so forth) should be included in all workshop announcements. It is most important to highlight the objectives and teaching strategies so potential participants can determine if this is the workshop for them (7,17,21,22,43). Further, a clear statement of the objectives can help forestall disappointment and frustration resulting from misconceptions and unfulfilled expectations. For similar reasons, it is important to present clearly in the promotional materials the teaching strategies to be used, especially if the strategies are nontraditional such as microteaching or call for high risk taking such as Tavistock methods.

You will need to have several communications with participants prior to the workshop. These communications should become more detailed as you move from initial announcement, through preregistration and preworkshop activities, to registration at the workshop. Your final preworkshop communication should even include details such as likely climate, recreation possibilities, names and addresses of other participants, potential activities for participants' family members, specific directions from airport, interstate route, bus stations, etc. Planners of several of the STFM workshops found they had telephone contact at least once with each participant before the workshop. Often, participants had questions, workshop planners needed to remind them to send in their preworkshop activities, materials were lost in the mail, or last-minute cancellations occurred.

It is helpful to set a consistent tone in preworkshop contacts with participants and to maintain this tone throughout the workshop. An expectation of structure with high activity established through preworkshop contacts helps participants adapt to directed exercises, for instance, during the actual workshop. Bergquist and Phillips note, however, that if an expectation of structure is established early, it is hard to break (16). If you plan to be highly responsive to the changing needs of participants and conduct a very flexible workshop, communicate this tone early to your participants.

During the workshop, use teacher-learner contacts to increase participants' trust and comfort in the workshop setting. This will facilitate learning by providing a supportive environment in which participants may try out new behaviors and concepts (16). Exercises to build group cohesion are recommended (12) as well as less structured time, such as dinners or outings during which faculty and participants may interact. Each of the STFM workshops had get-togethers on the evening prior to the actual workshop. In each case, these were social hours with snacks and cocktails. While this is a common ice-breaker, it may be more desirable to devise initial gatherings that do not promote alcohol. One workshop had a particularly successful outing to an Amana community that served family-style meals and whose handcrafted items for sale stimulated conversation. Another workshop had a casino night, using only funny money, to facilitate participant interest and camaraderie.

Be sensitive to participants' need for free time. When a workshop is of short duration (two–four days), participants can generally tolerate intensive, consistent interactions. If a workshop is longer than three days, it is necessary to leave some time unscheduled so participants can assimilate material and rest. Even though participants are highly motivated, after three days, fatigue and "oversaturation" disrupt learning (16). The STFM workshops showed a consistent pattern of high energy and alertness among participants during the first days and before noon during the later days (11,12). It may be wise to keep these observations in mind when scheduling workshop activities.

After the workshop, you can provide support for participants, even from a distance, by maintaining some contact with them through learning contracts or more informal interactions. One STFM workshop spontaneously developed a network of comrades who meet once a year at national meetings and share their successes and failures as faculty members.

Summary

Select participants who are most likely to benefit from your workshop. Be consistent — before, during, and after the workshop — in maintaining contact with them.

Chapter 8

SPECIFY OBJECTIVES

RULES OF THUMB

- Establish objectives based on the goals of the workshop.
- Concentrate objectives in one of the major categories of faculty function: teaching skills, administrative skills, research skills.
- Write objectives in behaviorial terms that will help you determine whether participants achieved them.
- Establish objectives that can realistically be achieved at the workshop.
- Select workshop objectives that are related to each other so that the entire workshop constitutes a whole.
- Establish relevant and practical objectives.
- Alert participants to the objectives in the initial announcement and throughout the workshop.

SUPPORTING EVIDENCE

As discussed in Chapter 5, needs assessment results are used to state the general purpose — or desired outcomes — for your workshop. Goal statements such as the following are useful in initial planning:

This workshop will help faculty members increase their
- research abilities, or
- administrative abilities, or
- teaching abilities.

Such broad statements communicate your goals to sponsors and funding sources, they identify the general area of faculty need you plan to address, they suggest the resources you will likely need, and they identify the content to be covered.

However, more specific statements of the abilities participants can expect to acquire as a result of attending your workshop are needed for the next stages of planning the workshop. Statements of expected learning outcomes, or instructional objectives as they are commonly called, are derived from broad goal statements. These objectives serve as your primary guides in selecting faculty and participants, choosing teaching strategies, and constructing evaluations.

An objective is . . . a statement describing a proposed change in a learner—a statement of what the learner is to be like when he has successfully completed a learning experience (44, p. 3).

Untold pages have been used to extoll the merits of instructional objectives. The *Educational Index* lists over 600 such references published during the early 1970s. The predominant opinion expressed in these articles is that instructional objectives are a critical element in any effective learning situation (44-66).

Rovin and Packer state the case for objectives as follows: "Learning occurs best when guided by a system of well-defined, attainable goals or objectives toward which the [teaching strategies] are directed. Without objectives, teaching becomes disorganized, students cannot separate the relevant from the irrelevant, and [evaluation is often impossible or meaningless]. The effectiveness of even the best teaching is seriously compromised if the students cannot see the purpose of the teaching or understand what is expected of them" (62, p. 497).

Gronlund succinctly lists the advantages of stating the purpose of an instructional session in terms of learning outcomes or instructional objectives (64, p.4):

- It provides direction for the instructor, and it clearly conveys his instructional intent to others.
- It provides a guide for selecting the subject matter, the teaching methods, and the materials to be used during instruction.
- It provides a guide for constructing tests and other instruments for evaluating student achievement.

Popham and Baker find yet a fourth benefit of using objectives: "A particularly important advantage of precisely stated objectives is that by removing the ambiguity of his instructional goals the teacher can often be in a better position to decide on the *worth* of his objectives" (63, p. 12).

WRITING OBJECTIVES

If you're not sure where you're going, you're liable to end up someplace else— and not even know it (44, p. vii).

Clearly, delineating the instructional objectives for your workshop is a crucial task. But exactly how do you go about writing objectives? That assignment is always a challenge. You must select, from your knowledge of a content area and the results of the needs assessment, a limited number of realistic, relevant abilities that individuals should acquire through participating in your workshop. If that isn't challenging enough, you must also write objectives in such a way that others, after reading them, will understand what abilities you intend to develop in the participants.

Fortunately, several slim texts, entertaining as well as instructive, are available to explain how to write objectives. The following are some titles:

• *Establishing Instructional Goals* (63)
• *Stating Behavioral Objectives for Classroom Instruction* (64)
• *Preparing Instructional Objectives* (44)
• *A Comprehensive Framework for Instructional Objectives* (65)

Each explains the steps necessary to refine workshop goals into specific behavioral statements that describe the abilities participants should acquire in your workshop. Because the mechanics of writing objectives are so well presented in these books, the instructions will not be repeated here.

One caveat, however, is in order: Don't fall into the trap of trying to outline every bit of knowledge, skill, or attitude your workshop could possibly produce. Let the main uses of objectives determine how detailed or extensive your objectives should be. Focus on a limited set of objectives (1) to guide your planning and (2) to meaningfully relate your instructional intentions to others. Put simply, a meaningful objective is reliable; it accurately "conveys to others a picture [of what a successful learner will be like] identical to the picture the writer has in mind" (44, p. 10).

Gronlund has devised a practical system of stating meaningful objectives (64). First, he says, refine goals into a limited set of "general objectives"—say six to twelve. Then further define each by a few "specific objectives." For example, one STFM workshop had as its goal "increasing participants' research abilities." This goal was further refined into six general objectives and associated specific objectives as shown below. Each of the general objectives could be defined by innumerable specific behaviors. However, the behaviors listed under each general objective are sufficient to guide workshop faculty in planning and to tell potential participants what specific learning they can expect from the workshop.

To say what one means by a goal is neither to reduce the importance of the goal or its profundity. . . . The act of writing it down means merely that what was once secret is now open for inspection and improvement (67, p. 35).

GENERAL AND SPECIFIC OBJECTIVES FOR WORKSHOP WITH GOAL OF:
INCREASING PARTICIPANTS' RESEARCH ABILITIES*

After participating in the workshop each participant will be able to do the following:
1. Refine a general research question including
    a.   Stating a general research question
    b.   After listing the variables that need to be measured to answer the research question, citing a method for measuring each variable, listing the resources required, and estimating the feasibility of measuring each variable
    c.   Restating the general research question as a more specific feasible question, i.e. a refined research question
    d.   Formulating a hypothesis that might represent a reasonable answer to the refined research question, and that the data of the study could support or fail to support
2. Create a research design including
    a.   Identifying three basic study designs and citing a function and limitation of each
    b.   Identifying four major problem areas in the structural design of studies and suggesting ways to deal with these
3. Develop a sampling plan including
    a.   Distinguishing between a sample and a population or a universe
    b.   Detecting ambiguities and/or inconsistencies between samples and the population they purport to represent
    c.   Distinguishing appropriate from inappropriate uses of tests

---

*Taken from STEM Research Workshop, Coronado, California, May 4-6, 1978. Stephen H. Gehlbach, M.D., Coordinator. Duke University, Durham, North Carolina.

of statistical significance (this does not include selection of particular tests of significance)

4. Discuss sample size including
    a. Describing the effects of increasing or decreasing sample size on the interpretation of results
    b. Identifying the considerations that are germane to the determination of sample size
    c. Consulting knowledgeably with a statistician in order to determine a reasonable sample size
5. Anticipate results including
    a. Using multiple fictitious tables and graphs to display likely results of practice studies
    b. Critiquing the fictitious presentations of others with respect to three items:
        finding ambiguities in research questions
        finding multiple interpretations of results
        finding omissions of data that limit the interpretations
    c. Explicitly stating expectations of study results
    d. Stating the value of the literature review as a means to
        begin with more informed expectations
        identify additional variables to consider
        identify other possibilities for design, analysis, or display of data
6. Choose a method of data collection including
    a. Listing the major types of data collection
    b. Discussing advantages and disadvantages of each type

CONTENT OF YOUR OBJECTIVES

This guidebook does not advocate certain objectives over others for your workshop. The content of your objectives should be determined by the needs of your participants as revealed through your needs assessment. However, the following general advice, culled from the sources cited, is offered:

- Cater to the specific needs of your participants and devise objectives that relate to the specific, immediate problems participants face back home (7,10,15,16,21,23,24,68).
- It may be best to focus on only one of the faculty roles (teacher, administrator, scholar/researcher) in any one workshop (12).
- Include objectives related to theory (e.g. education, learning, administration, statistics) but tie theory tightly to practical, concrete examples (9,20,24).

- Set forth only a limited number of objectives that can be realistically accomplished in the given time (10,21,22).
- Interrelate objectives of all parts of the workshop so that the entire experience constitutes a whole (15,22).

Recall that objectives serve the important function of clearly communicating the purpose for your workshop to others. Thus, it is important to refer to the workshop's goals and objectives in promotional materials, during initial workshop sessions and throughout the workshop, on evaluation forms, and in reports about the workshop. The objectives you choose also provide the basis for further workshop planning such as selecting teaching strategies, which is the focus of the next chapter.

Chapter 9

SELECT TEACHING STRATEGIES

RULES OF THUMB

- Select teaching strategies after considering the following:
  Participants' experience
  Type of objectives
  Instructors' preferences
  Available resources (instructors, materials, equipment, etc.)
  Desirability of illustrating a variety of strategies

- Emphasize preferred teaching strategies:
  Brief lectures or demonstrations
  Focused small group discussion
  Structured practice
          . . . all with plentiful feedback

- Appropriately illustrate what you are teaching.
- Consider using preworkshop materials to prepare participants for workshop activities.
- Integrate teaching strategies by considering such things as the following:
  Time duration
  Room requirements
  Pace
  Overall cohesiveness

- Use ready-made materials as much as possible.
- Rehearse the entire workshop.

SUPPORTING EVIDENCE

The most appropriate way to teach teachers is a question that remains unanswered in spite of the mountains of books and journal articles describing effective teaching. There are some major lines of convergence in the research nonetheless. In their in-depth summary of research related to teacher training, Peck and Tucker found that a systems approach to teacher education, often called "instructional design," substantially improves teaching effectiveness. Basically, a systems approach consists of the following steps (69, p. 943):

1. Precise specification of the behavior that is the objective of the learning experience
2. Carefully planned training procedures aimed explicitly at those objectives
3. Measurement of the results of the training in terms of the behavioral objectives
4. Feedback to the learner and the instructor of the observed results
5. Reentry into the training procedure
6. Measurement again of the results following the repeated training

Step 1, the importance of clearly stating your workshop objectives, was covered in Chapter 8. This chapter focuses on selecting appropriate training procedures and discusses (1) factors affecting choice of teaching strategies, (2) preferred teaching strategies, (3) examples of combining several teaching strategies, (4) aids for teaching, and (5) consultants.

FACTORS AFFECTING CHOICE OF TEACHING STRATEGIES

Ideally, teaching strategies should maximize participants' chances for achieving the instructional objectives. The specific strategies chosen for your workshop participants will depend on the following factors.

Participants' Experience as Faculty Members and Workshop Participants

A seasoned faculty member or one who is quite familiar with the workshop format adapts most easily to various teaching strategies. Experienced faculty are more comfortable with teaching strategies that require active participation, such as role playing, than participants who are novice faculty members experiencing their first faculty development workshop.

Type of Objectives

The type of objectives (knowledge, skill, or attitude) or level of objectives (from simple recall to technical mastery) for your workshop influence your choice of teaching strategy. For example, if your workshop is designed to change attitudes you will need to use activities that build trust in order to allow participants to openly explore values. On the other hand, if your focus is on training participants to conduct effective demonstrations, you would strive to include exemplary demonstration techniques as part of your teaching strategies.

Instructors' Preferences and Abilities

Understandably, people like to do what they think they do well. Try to capitalize on individual instructors' capabilities and preferences when selecting teaching strategies. Using a dynamic, demonstrative lecturer as a small group leader may not be the best use of talent, for instance.

Availability of Resources

The availability of rooms, buildings, equipment, support personnel, time, and money can greatly influence the pool of teaching strategies from which you may choose. The repeated movement of large groups to small groups requires that many small rooms as well as a large room be constantly available. Techniques such as microteaching and trigger films require several video setups and media personnel to assure their errorless operation. Microteaching is discussed below under "Preferred Teaching Strategies." The trigger films technique uses a very short, two- to three-minute, high impact vignette to elicit emotions and discussion from learners. A trigger film plunges the learner into a realistic problem and provides substance for active discussion (70).

Desirability of Illustrating a Variety of Strategies

Of course, you will appropriately illustrate what you are teaching. For example, if you're teaching participants the use of various types of questions and feedback, you will want to demonstrate both activities in your workshop. Your workshop probably has instructors who can expertly model several teaching strategies (such as lecture, small group discussion, role playing, etc.) as well as the apt use of questioning, demonstration, or media. Taking advantage of the full range of faculty talents enables you to unobtrusively model a variety of strategies, as well as provide some change of pace. Variety in teaching strategies, however, must be balanced against participants' tolerance for constantly adjusting their learning styles.

PREFERRED TEACHING STRATEGIES

Given the constraining factors discussed above, the following research results should be considered in selecting teaching strategies for a workshop. The results presented here are, at best, a keyhole glimpse of the literature on teacher training. The intent of this section is to give you an understanding, through selected references, of prominent findings and directions of current research. For a complete summary of the research in this area the reader is referred to the *Second Handbook of Research on Teaching* (71). Also, a useful list of indications and contraindications for many types of instruction is listed in *Taxonomy of Teaching Practices* (72).

Learning by Doing

Many programs for training teachers include a component of learning by doing, that is, they provide the teachers-in-training with an opportunity for practice teaching. Traditional "practice teaching," however, does not have good effects consistently. In fact, the effect of throwing a novice teacher into a teaching situation without adequate guidance often results in that teacher's developing undesirable teaching behaviors. Peck and Tucker describe a study by Matthews that investigated student teacher behaviors over three years. Matthews found that after the student teaching experience, the novice teachers became "more restrictive of student behaviors, they devoted an increasing proportion of their time to stating facts or their own opinions, . . . showed less acceptance and less clarification of student ideas, and the frequency and length of student response to their questions decreased" (69, p. 969).

Fortunately, these undesirable results can be largely avoided if the practice experience is clearly defined and structured. Currently enjoying widespread success in this area is a system called microteaching. Microteaching involves *real* teaching, but the complexities of a normal teaching situation are reduced by limiting class size, content, and time. Each microteaching session focuses on one specific teaching task or skill, for example, demonstration. The session is observed and usually videotaped, so that the trainee-teacher can receive immediate feedback from several sources: trainees, supervisor, and tape. This feedback can be immediately translated into practice as the trainee reteaches shortly after the critique (73).

The effects of this highly focused kind of practice teaching are impressive. Emmer and Millett investigated the effectiveness of a series of microteaching units and found that the experimental group performed significantly better than the control group on three out of four dimensions measured: determining student readiness, motivating students, and evaluating student responses. There was no difference in the dimension of clarifying the objectives (74).

Peck and Tucker report also a study by Davis and Smoot where it was found that student teachers going through a microteaching lab, as compared to a control group, "used more divergent questions, did more probing, less information giving, and elicited more pupil questions and statements. [Further,] they were more supportive, more clarifying, less procedural and less nonsubstantive in their remarks. The variety of their teaching methods increased significantly, as well" (69, p. 952).

Similar results have been found whether the student teachers were novice or experienced, taught first-grade math or college architecture, or taught in the United States or the Phillipines (73).

Writers on faculty development who address learning by doing, and specifically the use of simulation or real teaching with video-tape feedback, report that participants believe it to be a most effective teaching strategy (20-22,68,75,76). Similarly, participants in the STFM workshops that used microteaching rated it an effective and enjoyable technique. One workshop used a modified micro-teaching strategy in that participants brought a brief videotape of teaching activity with them to the workshop. Workshop faculty reviewed the tapes and gave written feedback and suggestions to the participants.

Discussion/Lecture/Demonstration

Millett studied four methods for preparing secondary teachers: unstructured discussion, oral instruction on how to teach the material, videotape demonstration of how to teach the material, and a combination of oral instruction and videotape demonstration (77). In an investigation of later classroom behavior, demonstration plus discussion was found to be the most effective training procedure, while unstructured discussion was the least effective. Likewise, Wedberg found that using a structured lecture along with tapes and experiences was most effective (78). Centra reports that small classes and discussion groups are most effective for the goals of retention, application, problem solving, attitude change, and motivation for learning (28). Finally, several faculty development researchers state that they prefer and/or their participants highly rate the discussion component of workshops (8,22,75).

Feedback

Steinen writes that each of three models for providing feedback increases skills, when performance of an experimental group is compared with a control group receiving no feedback (79). The three types of feedback he considers are (1) feedback from fellow student teachers, (2) from pupils, and (3) from oneself. Research consistently confirms the effectiveness of giving teachers objective feedback about specific aspects of their teaching behavior. Most evidence indicates, however, that teachers use such feedback to make changes in their teaching style only if another person participates in the feedback session (69). Findings of faculty development programs also show the importance of feedback to participants (10,15).

Readings

It is recommended that carefully selected readings be used as often as possible (9,10,68,80). Having participants read assigned materials in preparation for the workshop can serve to bring participants to an initial common understanding of basic knowledge and language. In addition, it saves precious workshop time for more interactive strategies, such as discussion or microteaching. The instructors, however, need to anticipate that some participants will come unprepared or even disenthralled, being unable to see the relevance of the materials to their particular teaching situation.

In addition to presession readings, it is suggested that a bibliography and list of consultants be provided after the workshop for participants' future reference.

Applying These Strategies

If you are unfamiliar with how to use these preferred teaching strategies, consult your education library or contact an educational consultant. You will find an abundance of excellent articles, books, films, and experts on every aspect of teaching, from preparing overhead transparencies to conducting a microteaching session. Often materials or consultants focus on a particular type of faculty. For example, *Teaching in Medical Schools* (81) by Holcomb and Gardner and the Teaching Improvement Project at the University of Kentucky (Lexington) address basic teaching practices such as lecture and demonstration but draw all their examples from the health professions.

In summary, preferred teaching strategies include brief lectures or demonstrations, focused discussion, and structured practice — all with plentiful feedback.

EXAMPLES OF COMBINING SEVERAL TEACHING STRATEGIES

There is no "best combination" or "ideal number" of teaching strategies. All of the STFM workshops used three or more of the strategies described above and other strategies such as trigger films, self-administered tests, and role playing. The following are three examples that may help you begin to structure and combine strategies for your workshop.

One of the STFM workshops used a skillful blend of prereading, then lecture or demonstration, followed either by small group discussion or learning by doing. Planners prepared written materials on the topic of writing objectives and mailed them to participants before the workshop. At the workshop, participants were reminded of the readings and given a short lecture on objectives that reviewed and expanded on the readings. Participants then were assigned to small groups where they were given the task of writing objectives on a given subject, utilizing the principles outlined in the readings and lectures.

Another workshop had a session devoted to learning how to prepare and conduct an effective demonstration. Before the workshop, participants were sent a self-instructional module on demonstrations and directed to (1) pick a demonstration topic that could be given in fifteen minutes, (2) begin to develop the objectives for the demonstration, and (3) locate and bring to the workshop any necessary props for conducting the demonstration. Five days before the workshop, the faculty member who would lead their small group called to remind them of the task and offer assistance. The final day of the workshop, the steps of an effective demonstration were reviewed through large group discussion, resulting in a checklist. With the checklist in hand, participants watched three short trigger films (three–eight minutes) illustrating disastrous and excellent demonstrations in the health care setting. A brief large group discussion followed each film. The group then divided into its functioning small groups and, again using the checklist, rated each others' microteaching demonstrations.

An STFM workshop on research covered nine topics using a three-part instructional sequence and sample research studies. In the first part of the sequence, a brief formal presentation was made by a faculty member, often involving participation by the total group. Immediately after the presentation, each participant worked individually for a few minutes on a task related to the topic. Then participants met in small groups to work on a task related to the topic. (Six or seven participants were randomly assigned to each group, and each group had an assigned faculty member. Group composition remained the same throughout the entire workshop.)

Participants had three sample research studies on which to apply the steps in research presented in each topic: a large group study, a small group study, and an individual study. The large group and small group studies were devised by participants once the workshop was under way. In an early session on formulating and refining a research question, the total group, with the help of the faculty presenter, identified a common research interest and refined it to a research question on continuity of patient care. Called the large group study, this example then served as the case-in-point for all future faculty presentations. During the small group sessions on formulating and refining a research question, each small group identified a research question of common interest to its members that then became the focus for all their subsequent group activities. Small groups' studies varied from investigating the effects on obesity of several patient education strategies to comparing the practice patterns of residency trained family physicians to nonresidency trained family physicians.

Finally, all participants were asked to come prepared with a research proposal that would be carried out on their return home. They were expected to keep their individual research proposal in mind during the presentations and small group exercises. On the last day of the workshop, each participant explained how the topics covered in the workshop applied to his or her own study that was then discussed and critiqued by the small group.

Each of the above meldings of teaching strategies began with the coordinator alone, or with others, working out possible combinations on paper. Doubtless, none of the above final outcomes closely resembles these original thoughts, but you have to begin somewhere to draft the master plan for your workshop. So begin — with plenty of scratch paper — to outline alternative combinations and intertwinings of appropriate strategies and workshop segments. For each workshop segment, carefully note the following:

- time duration
- room requirements
- equipment/material requirements
- participant groupings
- faculty requirements
- responsible or predominant faculty person
- pace, focus, teaching strategy change
- overall cohesiveness and balance

Do not attempt to solidify the workshop structure early. This is the time for flexibility and creativity. Be sure also to prepare a contingency plan because it will allow you to modify strategies during the workshop in response to changing circumstances, e.g. participants become fatigued, have difficulty mastering an objective, express special interest in pursuing a topic further. Try out your "paper program" on others. Certainly, include all your committee members, faculty, and consultants.

Once you think you have a master plan laid out, it is time to rehearse. Your participants have paid good money and given up valuable time to attend your workshop and you want to avoid all the little calamities that can occur in an unrehearsed production — dropped props, poor timing, lost lighting, burned bulbs, unanticipated and unwanted ad libs, and *bad reviews*. To quote Davis and McCallon, "Rehearsing [a workshop] is an activity both simple and crucial" (29, p.185).

To avoid calamities—rehearse

Your dress rehearsal should include a review of all materials (books, tapes, slides, films, props), strategies (lectures, demonstrations, discussions), rooms and chair arrangements, handouts, and so forth. You will find that some of your faculty, particularly consultants, will balk at taking part in a rehearsal. Nevertheless, be firm, cajole, coax them along. Admittedly, it feels a bit uncomfortable rehearsing your presentation with planted jokes and premeditated questions in front of two or three colleagues who are role playing participants. But there never fails to be a payoff in such an activity, be it the rude discovery that a consultant has changed his or her presentation from what you had previously discussed or merely an increase in precision and camaraderie among faculty.

Try to conduct your rehearsal from the beginning with each faculty member practicing his or her part, or crucial portions thereof. Pay close attention to possibly troublesome areas such as teaching aids, team teaching, and transitions to the next presenter or activity. If you have consultants from out of town who cannot participate in rehearsal, request their written presentation and materials be sent to you to be played by another at rehearsal. Meanwhile, other faculty should role play participants—anticipating questions, confusions, distractions, etc.

Better to muff your lines or make a fool of yourself during rehearsal than when the curtain rises on the real show.

Actually, rehearsals can be a great deal of fun and can reduce anxiety among faculty, particularly if your faculty have not presented a workshop together before.

AIDS FOR TEACHING: HANDBOOKS, TEXTS, NEWSLETTERS, CONSULTANTS

Some excellent materials are available for commonly taught workshop subjects, allowing you to focus your creative efforts on topics unique to your setting. Listed below is a sample of such materials. Since this is only a sample of available materials and because, undoubtedly, others will be available by the time you read this, it is suggested that you inquire about other books, tapes, modules, and consultants beyond those listed below. A complete reference for each of the items appears in the Bibliography.

Handbooks
Educational Handbook (43)

This handbook (third revision, English text) was written by the educational director of the World Health Organization specifically for teachers of health sciences at all levels and health administrators with staff supervision responsibilities. It contains theoretical content and exercises on objectives, planning of teaching/learning activities, evaluation, and tests and measurement techniques. The handbook has many useful ideas and handouts as well as "critical" pages printed in large type for ease in making transparencies for overhead projection. Although the handbook's unusual organization can be irritating at times, the persistent reader is abundantly rewarded by valuable handouts, many health care examples, and a refreshing world-wide perspective.

A Handbook for Faculty Development (16)

This book was written for the broader audiences of non-health related faculty. It has many practical suggestions and handouts as well as guidelines for actually doing faculty development. The book begins with a brief overview of faculty development and concludes with a section suggesting a number of ways colleges and universities can develop and sustain their own faculty development programs. The middle sections have separate chapters on such things as teaching styles, observation skills, course designs, teaching strategies (lectures, small group discussion, microteaching), etc. Each chapter has an introduction followed by related instruments, handouts, and exercises.

Planning, Conducting, and Evaluating Workshops (29)

This book focuses on adult education through workshops and has two sections devoted to teaching strategies. "Methods Primer" presents commonly used teaching strategies for workshops; "Warm-up Methods" has practical suggestions for "breaking the ice."

Research Workbook: A Guide for Initial Planning of Clinical, Social and Behavioral Research Projects (82)

This workbook is a do-it-yourself manual for inexperienced researchers that has been found useful with family practice faculty.

Texts

Drawn from the entire body of literature on adult education, the following specifically address the teaching of adult students of the health sciences. While these books are in the style of the traditional text with no handouts or exercises, they have many chapters that would serve well as readings.

> *Improving Teaching in Medical Schools: A practical handbook* (81)
>
> *Teaching in the Health Professions*(83)
>
> *Clinical Education for the Allied Health Professions* (84)
>
> *Evaluating Clinical Competence in the Health Professions* (85)
>
> *Teaching and Learning in Medical School* (86) (This is an old and now occasionally incomplete book, but the principles presented remain sound.)

Newsletters

Several newsletters exist that will apprise you of newly written articles and books on developing faculty as well as inform you of faculty development conferences and actions. One such newsletter is entitled *Faculty Development and Evaluation in Higher Education.** *Exchange* is another faculty development newsletter published by the Center for Faculty Evalution and Development in Higher Education.†

Centers/Tapes/Films

Finally, there are consultants and centers that can provide you with modules, films, or videotapes, or conduct the entire workshop. The Teaching Improvement Project, headquartered at the University of Kentucky in Lexington and other regional sites, is a particu-

---

*Published quarterly, it is available from Dr. Albert B. Smith, editor, 3930 N.W. 35th Place, Gainesville, Florida 32605.

†The Center's address is 1627 Anderson Avenue, Box 3000, Manhattan, Kansas 66502.

larly valuable source for materials and videotapes specifically designed for the development of health professions faculty through workshops. Also, the Center for Faculty Evaluation and Development in Higher Education, Manhattan, Kansas, can provide help particularly oriented towards faculty who are not in health professions. Appendix XIV lists consultants you may wish to contact for further information. Both Gaff's *Faculty Renewal* (3) and Bergquist and Phillip's *Handbook for Faculty Development* (16) contain lists of centers for faculty development that you may want to consult. Also, Gaff's *Professional Development: A guide to resources* (87) lists such things as journals, newsletters, and centers, and provides as well an annotated bibliography of the literature on faculty development and evaluation.

Summary

This chapter is scattered with both good news and bad news. While the research on teaching can direct you to many effective teaching strategies, you are limited in your choice by factors such as available instructors and facilities. Also, there seems to be no pat formula for combining these strategies into a two-four day workshop. But there are many sources for already made modules, tapes, and handouts. Further, there are numerous consultants and centers available to contact for help.

Chapter 10

ESTABLISH EVALUATION

RULES OF THUMB

• Establish evaluation procedures to assess whether participants achieved the goals and objectives of the workshop.
• Consider collecting other information through the evaluation, e.g. participant demographics, reactions to the workshop setting.
• Provide a mechanism for assessing participants' learning during the workshop.
• Provide frequent opportunities during the workshop for informal and formal feedback from participants and instructors.
• Conduct a long-term follow-up evaluation to measure the impact of the workshop on participants' skills in their home setting.
• If possible, use an external evaluator to conduct the evaluation.

SUPPORTING EVIDENCE

There is a strong temptation to put off thinking about evaluation. After all, it often gets administered at the end of the workshop or even months later. Right? Wrong! It can be the first thing you do at a workshop. Further, it is the critical step that can provide information about every other component of your workshop. Thus, this is definitely not the time to get lazy (skip evaluation) or worse, sloppy (whip up some half-baked questions the night before). After all the effort you, your committee, faculty, and participants have or will put into your workshop, at the very least you will want to know if participants really did gain those abilities you were aiming for. If you or your sponsor plan to rerun your workshop or one similar to it, it would be most helpful to know answers to questions such as these: Were the goals "on target?" Which teaching strategies worked best? Which presentations need to be redesigned? How effective were your teachers? How appropriate was the timing? What suggestions were made about accommodations?

A well-designed evaluation provides data that can help you answer these questions. *Well-designed,* however, is an important key word. A well-designed evaluation addresses your specific questions and gathers information about them in a comprehensive and accurate manner. Evaluation data that have these characteristics are said to be reliable and valid.* No matter how "hard" and official your evaluation results look when typed up in a table, you will not know how much weight to give them in making decisions about your workshop unless you know the extent to which your data are valid and reliable.

Unfortunately, unlike the topic of objectives, evaluation is not amenable to quick mastery through brief, entertaining texts. If you are unfamiliar with designing an evaluation, *The Program Evaluation Kit* (89-95) provides step-by-step help through eight easy-to-understand "how to" books. Or, you may wish to contact an evaluation consultant instead. Your local college of education, office of educational research and development, or one of the faculty development consultants listed in Appendix XIV can help you find an evaluation consultant.

Whether you are going to be constructing your own evaluation or working with a consultant, your first step is to identify questions you have about the workshop. These questions will provide the foundation on which to build your evaluation instrument(s). The questions can be grouped into three main categories, for each of which there is a corresponding type of evaluation.

- Needs assessment (see Chapter 5) is used to choose appropriate goals for a program.
- Formative evaluation determines the effectiveness of a program while it is being conducted.
- Summative evaluation assesses the overall effectiveness of a program once it is completed.

You will probably want to use all three types of evaluation. Keep this in mind though: The kinds of information you want about your workshop will determine which types of evaluation you establish. *These decisions must be made before the workshop begins.*

---

*Reliability refers to the consistency of your data. A reliable evaluation, if administered a second time, would yield the same data about your workshop as the first time. Validity refers to the accuracy of your data. A valid evaluation gives you the true story about your workshop.

The following paragraphs offer a rationale for and illustrations of summative and formative evaluations.

SUMMATIVE EVALUATION

Conducting a needs assessment to establish relevant, achievable objectives for your particular group of participants was discussed in Chapter 5. A needs assessment has another use also: to mark participants' abilities as they enter the workshop, against which you can contrast their abilities after they complete the workshop. Comparing preprogram to postprogram abilities after the workshop ends is one form of summative evaluation. "Pre-post" is the evaluator's shorthand term for this testing plan.

Before- and after-workshop measures of participants' abilities and workshop effectiveness were used in most of the STFM projects. One workshop used all the following pre-post measures: an objective test of achievement relative to the workshop objectives, a test of participant confidence with respect to the workshop objectives, and a videotape of a precepting session.

The external or third-party evaluators for the STFM study developed a standard pre-post self-assessment called a Faculty Activities Rating (FAR). With the FAR, participants judged what they perceived to be their level of performance on a number of general faculty activities and rated as well the importance they gave to each activity. (See Appendix X.) Since this instrument was used at all the STFM workshops, planners were able to compare participants' perceived progress across workshops. You may wish to use the FAR and compare your participants' ratings to the ratings of individuals who participated in the STFM-sponsored workshops (12,14).

A comment should be made about possible limitations inherent in the pre-post self-assessment design used in the STFM study. It may be that the standard against which participants measured their ability level changed as a result of attending the workshop. Recent studies have shown that such a response shift bias has occurred in the evaluation of some programs (96,97,98). In most instances the shift resulted in a more conservative estimate of the effect of the workshop than other measures such as objective pre-post tests or self-report of both pre and post abilities after the workshop (then-post). Thus, had a response shift occurred in the STFM study, it is likely that it resulted in an underestimate of the workshop's effectiveness. However, these recent findings suggest that when participants' self-assessment is used to evaluate the effectiveness of a workshop, it may be best to use a then-post design to avoid response shift bias. An example of how one STFM workshop planner modified the FAR to a then-post design is found in Appendix XI. Appendix XII is an example of a postworkshop assessment.

Certainly, one conducts a workshop with the hope that it will have enduring effects on participants. Long-term summative evaluation must be used if you want to know the *real effect* your workshop had on participants. Long-term evaluation can take the form of interviews, mailed questionnaires, reports, or objective tests. Nine months after the STFM workshops, the third-party evaluators conducted a follow-up assessment and found that the workshops did have significant enduring effects on participants' faculty behaviors (14).

If you want to assess retention of behavior learned during your workshop, objective evaluation methods provide the most valid and reliable results. Objective, long-term evaluation must be conducted long enough after the workshop to ensure that results indeed indicate enduring behavior.

FORMATIVE EVALUATION

Formative evaluation collects information about a program while the program is occurring. Changes based on this information can keep the workshop "on target" for participants. For instance, you might modify objectives, change teaching strategies, adjust pacing, and so forth. Making changes en route, of course, requires very adaptable faculty and facilities. Nevertheless, since your overriding workshop goal is to meet the needs of participants, you should be prepared to make some midcourse adjustments to assure a smooth-running, effective workshop.

The STFM workshops all used some type of formative evaluation, varying from informal questioning of participants and objective quizzes to daily written feedback from participants about their perceptions of the workshop and suggestions for change.

One caveat is in order. In a three-day workshop there is little time for major revision in response to formative evaluations. Therefore, do not give participants the impression that you can perform major program revisions while they sleep. One of the STFM workshops built into its design a "safety valve" that you may find useful. Optional, unstructured night sessions were scheduled in a resource room that was staffed by workshop personnel and others. It contained a portable mini-library of resource books, a computer terminal, and audiovisual equipment with teaching tapes. If an unforeseen need arose, staff asked interested participants to pursue that topic with them in the evening. If additional staff or resources were necessary, a staff person was immediately dispatched to make arrangements for the evening sessions. For short workshops, thorough trouble shooting beforehand and planning for the unexpected are essential to avoid major problems when the workshop is running.

EXTERNAL EVALUATORS

Several coordinators of the STFM workshops found that the presence of an external evaluator* was an added stimulus to provide the best possible workshop. Also, the "outside" perspective provided by the external evaluator in his or her report was found most helpful. Thus, you may want to arrange for a third-party evaluator.

ALTERNATIVE APPROACHES

You may have noticed that this section on evaluation favors using evaluation models that measure workshop success by assessing how well participants accomplished its stated objectives. This bias toward goal or objective-based evaluation parallels the systems approach to workshop design promoted throughout this guidebook. In addition, objective-based evaluation is the model typically used by planners of faculty development workshops.

All the same, you should know that there are other approaches to evaluation that you may find useful. For example, Wergin, Mason, and Munson suggest that for some learners the effect of a workshop may simply be internal changes such as an increase in awareness of various faculty activities or an increase in willingness to question traditional strategies (7). Such changes as these are not often stated

---

*In the case of external evaluation, the workshop planners contract with an outside person or organization to assess the workshop. The external evaluator is not part of the workshop planning committee and has no part in the design or implementation of the workshop.

in the objectives and would go undetected by an objective-based evaluation. An evaluation approach that seeks unexpected outcomes, however, would pick up such changes. Some of these alternative approaches include Scriven's Goal-free Model, Stake's Responsive Approach, and the Adversary Model. The *Encyclopedia of Educational Evaluation* (26) briefly describes alternative approaches; *Educational Evaluation: Theory and Practice* (99) gives an in-depth description of common alternative models. Finally, the highly curious reader is referred to *The Handbook of Evaluation Research* (100).

Chapter 11

CHOOSE WORKSHOP SETTING

RULES OF THUMB

- Identify a location with few distractions.
- Utilize an area that will allow for "captive" participants.
- When choosing location, consider comfort, cost, meeting rooms, sleeping accommodations, food, and recreation.
- Meeting rooms should meet the following standards:

    Large enough to accommodate anticipated size of groups
    Amenable to planned activities
    Readily accessible
    Interchangeable as needed

- Arrange to have one site official designated as your liaison.
- Confirm all site arrangements in writing.

SUPPORTING EVIDENCE

It is now clear that we must take into account what the environment does to an organism (101, p. 16).

The environment is basic; more than anything else it determines the behavior of individuals (3, p. 75).

Given the importance of the environment, selecting a location for your workshop should not be a casually considered task, simply delegated to an assistant — "Call the convention center, schedule a hotel, reserve appropriate rooms." This is a task that deserves your attention. The major question to keep in mind when considering a potential workshop site is: Will these surroundings and facilities decrease or increase the effectiveness of the workshop? The best planned and most stimulating workshop can be significantly hampered by distracting and detracting elements of the environment.

One of the STFM workshop coordinators learned this fact the hard way. Only during the workshop did he discover that the traffic pattern for incoming flights to the local airport placed the deafening pride of Boeing aeronautics directly overhead every forty to sixty minutes! Don't underestimate the powerful impact of the environment.

Characteristics you should consider when selecting a site are discussed below. See Appendix XIII for a convenient survey form devised by Davis and McCallon (29) for recording critical features of a facility.

LOCATION OF WORKSHOP FACILITY

The workshop should take place in a setting free from distractions from within and far enough away from participants' home programs to discourage any routine communication. The STFM study found that a retreat setting with self-contained living/learning facilities best serves the social, psychological, and educational needs of participants. To quote Reineke and Welch, "The remote retreat setting not only promoted positive feelings but helped to establish a sense of psychological isolation which perhaps increased the participants' capacity to focus on the workshop objectives" (12, p. 59).

The ideal "remote retreat site" seems to be somewhere between the highly isolated, monasterylike setting and the swinging resort. Davis and McCallon talk about the difficulties with the monastic setting such as no phones and dormitory-style rooms (29). On the other hand, one STFM workshop was a near miss in a resort setting. This workshop — early May, sunny San Diego — occurred in a beautiful setting surrounded by beach, sail boats, and tennis courts. To participants snowbound for the previous six months, the allure of all this was irresistible. Although the days just before and after the workshop were filled with beautiful California weather, fortunately for the planners, the workshop days were cloudy, overcast, and drizzly.

APPROPRIATENESS OF CONFERENCE ROOMS

Match the rooms — capacity, layout, facilities, location, and comfort — with your teaching strategies and group size. This may sound obvious but if you don't keep this simple tenet in mind, you may find that site staff have placed your group in the most convenient room for *their* purposes instead, such as a large ballroom or outside atrium. Rooms should be optimal size—not so large that your group gets lost in them nor so small that participants must literally rub elbows. Optimal size, of course, varies with the number of participants and type of activity. To ascertain the appropriateness of a room's size, you may want to actually set up tables in the U-shape you had planned or try out the round tables you had thought of using for discussion groups, etc.

Conference rooms are usually rectangular or square, thus they can be arranged in a variety of ways, such as U-shaped, classroom, theater, corner buzz groups, and so on. Occasionally, rooms will have design features that greatly limit their use, such as narrow and long, L-shaped, multileveled, with large columns or other immovable elements. Steer clear of oddly constructed rooms.

The minimum facilities to look for in a conference room include sufficient three-prong outlets, adequate lighting with dimmers, conveniently placed doors, proper ventilation, and temperature control. Windows can be a plus or a minus. The beauty of the outdoors can add to your workshop, but note that bright sunlight can detract from visuals, heat a room, and glare in people's eyes. Further, an outside view can turn out to be a distraction if it includes handsome vacationers or curious passersby.

If you are using more than one room—for example, one large conference room with several smaller discussion rooms—try to get the small rooms close to the larger one. You don't want to break concentration or lose precious time, or worse, participants, by moving groups to distant rooms. If the smaller conference rooms are created via pull-out walls in the large conference room, plan in advance what to do with participants while the rooms are being "constructed." Similarly, try to locate at least your primary room so that it is away from the main flow of traffic but near restrooms, telephones, and drinking fountains.

Ideal furnishing will depend on your teaching strategies. Workshop facilities typically have available a variety of tables and chairs that can be placed anyway you wish. Do not hesitate to request exactly the furnishings and arrangements that will serve you best. Do they have padded chairs with arms rather than straight-back or folding chairs? Check for smooth surface tables for writing rather than layers of tablecloths. Do you need a table at the front for an overhead projector or one at the back for a slide projector? How about high rolling tables for videotape monitors? Finally, be sure to personally check each room set-up an hour before you'll use it. This is both a double check on the contractual agreements you made with the hotel or center, as well as a final opportunity to modify your advance plans in light of what's actually happened at the workshop.

You may not usually pay much attention to room appointments. Some learners even seem oblivious to their surroundings. Nevertheless, the appointments in a room that your participants will be spending literally days in can add a fine polish to their learning efforts, which in turn reflects well on planners and unobtrusively sets a climate of precision. A dull-looking room or one that is dirty and in disrepair says you condone sloppy work. That's not the message to transmit to participants who are trying to fine hone their faculty skills.

One facility the author recently used for a workshop had transformed what once was a stable into perfect rooms for a workshop for thirty-five participants. One wall was entirely windows equipped with Levelor brand shades that allowed filtered light or a panoramic view of a peaceful lake and farm country. The rooms, equipped with all the necessary facilities, were off-white throughout (walls, tables, carpet, chairs). Simply framed poster graphics were the only decoration. Tables were smooth-topped and provided with pads and pencils, water and coffee pitchers, and candies. Padded desk chairs on rollers accompanied them. Set apart from the rest of the facility, the major conference and discussion rooms were arranged in a spoke pattern with registration area, restrooms, phones, and refreshments in the center. To a one, participants (who had given up a beautiful July weekend to attend the conference) smiled broadly and visibly relaxed as they entered this redone stable. Before a word had been said, a great deal had been communicated to participants about the workshop's purpose, planners' expectations, and their willingness to make this a positive experience for participants.

GUEST ROOMS

Although participants will appreciate comfortable rooms to relax in after working hard all day, the cost of the rooms should not be exorbitant. However, you don't want complaints about accommodations to detract from the workshop. Check a sample of sleeping rooms (three or four) before negotiating with the site. Ask to see the best and the worst rooms. Keep in mind that most participants will want a private telephone to call home, would like a little "Today" and "Tonight" show to begin and end the day, and prefer double beds. Again, while luxury isn't necessary, expect comfort, cleanliness, and pleasant appointments.

FOOD

Menu choices should provide enough variety to satisfy most appetites since individuals with various tastes will be in attendance. Keep midday meals light and omit alcohol so that participants are refreshed, alert, and awake for afternoon activities. It's a good idea to eat lunch on site during one of your visits to personally assess food and service.

RECREATIONAL FACILITIES

With the current emphasis on physical fitness, participants appreciate a workshop site that provides a recreational alternative to drinking in a bar. Especially after an intensive day of learning while sitting, most participants welcome a little physical activity. Occasionally, participants will continue functioning as a group and spontaneously set up an activity such as volleyball. More often, however, participants break into small groups and take advantage of tennis courts, swimming pools, bike trails, or walking paths. Fortunately, many conference centers and hotels offer various recreational activities. If you do not see the facilities you had in mind, ask about what arrangements could be made with nearby health clubs or parks.

COST

The many items to consider in estimating the cost of a workshop site were discussed in Chapter 6. Once you have selected your workshop site, arrange to have one site official designated as your liaison. Be sure to confirm in writing all arrangements made. Recall that your workshop is only one of the many arrangements hotel or conference center managers negotiate everyday. It is easy for them to forget or confuse your plans with others. To avoid any mishaps, reiterate in a letter your discussions with them about the following:

- meeting room with schedules and setups
- refreshments for breaks
- meals (menu, time, number, billing)
- guest rooms (number, cost, reservation policy, billing, check-out time)
- audiovisuals
- space to store materials
- support capabilities (photocopying, typing, message service, laundry, medical care)
- parking
- special arrangements (tours, agreements with nearby health or country clubs)

Follow up in writing any changed arrangements. Two weeks before the workshop, personally contact the site official who has been handling your workshop plan to see if any last-minute problems have arisen.

GESTALT

Walk around the facility. Instead of focusing on specific components of the facility, pay attention to what the place feels like — party time, drudgery, professional? This is a hard one to put your finger on, but if a place doesn't say "workshop" to you it probably won't to your participants either. Small conference centers seem to set the appropriate mood most easily but a similar ambiance can be found in city hotels too. The American Academy of Family Practice and STFM frequently hold meetings and workshops in the Alameda Plaza in Kansas City, for instance. Unsolicited positive comments about this hotel are abundant from people who have attended meetings there. Even though it is a busy hotel in a relatively large city, it is close to other activities (parks, tennis, shopping), has good food, is always pleasant, comfortable, nicely appointed, plus its staff appear to be consistently coached in smiling service. Thus, even a hotel in a metropolitan area can serve as your "remote" setting.

APPENDICES

OUTLINE OF
FAMILY MEDICINE FACULTY ABILITIES*

I. Teaching role

A. The faculty member will design a residency curriculum to teach residents in family practice.
   1. Assesses needs of residents in area of expertise.
   2. Writes goal statements.
   3. Establishes educational objectives in a curriculum area.
   4. Assesses resources available within the curriculum to meet goals and objectives.
   5. Locates and uses sources of help in curriculum designing (educational specialists, curriculum content area specialists).
B. The faculty member will devise strategies and utilize effective methods for teaching residents.
   1. Writes instructional objectives in curriculum area from goals and educational objective statements.
   2. Allocates available resources efficiently to help residents meet instructional objectives.
   3. Devises specific strategies (experiences for the resident, teacher behaviors, time allotment, etc.) to help residents meet instructional objectives.
   4. Exhibits skill in using communicative techniques that aid resident learning (in lecture, small-group and one-on-one settings) — including audiovisual aids, persuasion, rapport, clarity of explanation, timing and pacing.
C. The faculty member will evaluate the learning of residents,

---

*Although this outline focuses on family medicine faculty and mentions residents as students, its content is applicable to higher education faculty and learners in any field.

Developed by Carole J. Bland, Ph.D., Department of Family Practice and Community Health, University of Minnesota, Minneapolis, Minnesota.

the skill of teachers (preceptors) and the adequacy of teaching strategies and methods.

    1. Devises tests of resident abilities in curriculum area.

    2. Analyzes test results.

    3. Utilizes certain statistical and experimental design methods to plan course, instructor and resident evaluations.

    4. Makes appropriate inferences from evaluation information and implements changes in teaching strategies and methods according to them.

D.   The faculty member will discover or devise personal support systems for evaluating and teaching and for designing curricula.

    1. Establishes personal rapport with residents.

    2. Hones teaching skills so as to be entertaining and brief as well as informative.

    3. Gives each resident personal help in learning when needed.

    4. Shares skills and teaching experiences with colleagues.

    5. Meets formal requirements for promotion and official recognition as a teacher (preceptor, professor).

    6. Sets personal teaching objectives and assesses own accomplishments against them.

II. Administrative role

A.   The faculty member will effectively utilize the authority structure.

    1. Describes the structure of the organization.

    2. Describes lines of authority.

    3. Identifies the power structure (who can get things done.)

    4. Efficiently uses available resources to meet own responsibilities (including delegating responsibility when appropriate).

    5. Utilizes lines of authority and the appropriate power structure to implement decisions.

B.   The faculty member will encourage and maintain the necessary flow of information through the organization.

    1. Identifies administrative information sources.

    2. Systematically obtains required information.

3. Organizes relevant information efficiently.
4. Maintains convenient store (file) of useful information.
5. Provides information as needed (responds to information requests and deadlines).

C. The faculty member will function effectively as a group member.
   1. Lists own committee responsibilities.
   2. Functions as a committee member (makes effective use of formal group procedures and informal group dynamics).
   3. Avails oneself of committee expertise to accomplish objectives.
   4. Follows through on committee tasks and ideas in own work.

D. The faculty member will discover or devise personal support systems for fulfilling administrative responsibilities.
   1. Offers administrative expertise and power to colleagues.
   2. Cheerfully and speedily provides help to those who require it.
   3. Seeks credit for own accomplishments and the accomplishments of others, when deserved.
   4. Participates in the social milieu of the organization.
   5. Volunteers to serve in arbitrator and liaison roles.

III. Academic role

A. The faculty member will upgrade and maintain personal competence in academic disciplines that contribute to family practice.
   1. Utilizes resources (especially colleagues) within own department to upgrade skills in less familiar areas of family practice disciplines.
   2. Reads journals and professional literature, attends rounds and conferences, and enrolls in academic courses and practica in the various disciplines of family practice.
   3. Practices own skills.
   4. Maintains contact with developments within the field of family practice and in related fields.

B. The faculty member will formulate adequate research ideas and critically review reports of research in family practice.

1. Formulates research ideas in acceptable research design formats.
2. Critically reviews research in the disciplines relating to family practice.
3. Locates and consults specialists in the design and interpretation of research (statisticians and clinical experts).

C. The faculty member will communicate information concerning the discipline of family practice.
1. Writes journal articles, position papers, and grant proposals.
2. Prepares and delivers interesting and informative presentations appropriate for conferences, rounds, meetings, and conventions.
3. Provides information in both formal and informal one-to-one situations (e.g. as an advisor, a colleague, and a subordinate).

D. The faculty member will discover or devise personal support systems for meeting academic responsibilities.
1. Seeks colleagues who recognize and appreciate own expertise.
2. Takes personal pride in and contributes to the recognition of the field of family practice by other medical specialists, academicians in related fields, patients, and the public.
3. Gains exposure to those whose recognition and appreciation is valued by volunteering to present papers, lead discussions, hold family medicine rounds, and chair meetings.

NEEDS ASSESSMENT QUESTIONNAIRE

FAMILY MEDICINE FACULTY DEVELOPMENT WORKSHOP

The following list of topics has been compiled from workshop applicants' responses to the question "What would you like to get out of this workshop?" and from our initial set of possible areas of interest.

We are asking that you rank the topics in order of your personal preference. The topics that are most highly ranked by participants will be covered during the workshop's "advanced skills presentation" periods. Please assign a rank of "1" to your MOST PREFERRED topic, "2" to the next most preferred topic, etc. If you have no interest in a topic at all, do not rank it.

RANK   *TOPIC*

_____   Designing a residency applicant selection system

_____   Residency curriculum development: scheduling activities

_____   Residency curriculum development: defining the content of Family Medicine

_____   Orienting new residents

_____   Preparing and delivering lectures

_____   Audio and video recording residents' performance

_____   Designing self-instructional units

_____   Interview training using Interpersonal Process Recall

_____   Behavioral science training methods

_____   Using simulation for instruction and evaluation

_____   Auditing patient care records to evaluate residents' performance

_____   Multiphasic in-training assessment of residents

_____   Designing patient record systems for ambulatory care

_____   Preparing a grant proposal

YOUR NAME AND ADDRESS: *RETURN WITH REGISTRATION FEE TO:*

---

* Developed by James A. Bobula, Ph.D., Duke-Watts Family Medicine Program, Durham, North Carolina.

FAMILY MEDICINE TEACHER TRAINING WORKSHOP: PREPARATORY MATERIALS (PERSONAL PREASSESSMENT AND EXERCISE)

If your first impulse upon looking at this stack of materials is to scream, **wait!** After reading this guide you should feel more relaxed.

The Assessments

The "Personal Preassessment" asks you to describe how confident you are right *now* with information or skills to be addressed in the workshop. Don't be surprised if some of the jargon is unfamiliar. If you understood it all, you'd probably be wasting your time coming to the workshop. You should be able to breeze through this task in a few minutes.

The "Assessment Exercise" puts you in the role of a faculty member reviewing objectives for a residency curriculum. Your review takes the form of answers to a standard set of inquiries about each of five objectives. An answer sheet is provided for recording your responses. Once again, you will not be asked to deal with any portions of this exercise involving terminology you find unfamiliar.

Please do not consult with colleagues or bother looking up educational literature. **Do the assessments before the other preparatory materials.**

The Instructions

The workshop will provide a structured environment for participants to share their experience in training family physicians. The instructions are intended to help you capture elements of your ex-

---

Developed by James A. Bobula, Ph.D., Duke-Watts Family Medicine Program, Durham, North Carolina. Copyright © 1977 by the Duke-Watts Family Medicine Program. All rights reserved. Reprinted by permission.

perience as a basis for certain workshop activities. Most of the instructions relate to activities that are *optional* so you may *skip* much
of what is requested. **Please be sure to follow the "required"**
instructions since they prepare you for sessions that are central to
the workshop.

PERSONAL PREASSESSMENT

*NAME:*_____

Instructions

This questionnaire lists each of the workshop's instructional objectives
and asks you to estimate the degree of confidence you have with respect
to the knowledge and / or skill specified.

Please read each objective carefully. Then circle the ONE response
code which best describes your present level of confidence.

Response Codes

VC for "very confident, secure in knowing that I have mastered this
objective."

C   for "confident that I can adequately deal with this objective."

N   for "no particular feelings about this objective at this time; I am not
definite in my level of confidence."

I   for "insecure, knowing that I would have a difficult time dealing
with this objective."

VI   for "very insecure, knowing that I definitely could not deal with
this objective."

?   for "I do not know what this objective means; the terminology is
unfamiliar or unclear to me."

Instructional Objectives

1. List at least ten skills or content areas of personal expertise.

    CONFIDENCE: VC C N I VI ?

2. Write a plan for an instructional unit (conference, self-instructional
    package, rotation, etc.) explicitly identifying instructional objec-
    tives stated in terms of learner behaviors.

    CONFIDENCE: VC C N I VI ?

3. Write a plan for an instructional unit explicitly identifying an
    instructional strategy for each objective, indicating alternative
    strategies in cases where learners should be given options.

    CONFIDENCE: VC C N I VI ?

4. Write a plan for an instructional unit explicitly identifying
    resources (personnel, patients, space, time, learning materials,
    finances, etc.) required for implementation.

    CONFIDENCE: VC C N I VI ?

5. Evaluate the appropriateness of an available instructional package for achieving specific objectives.

   CONFIDENCE: VC C N I VI ?

6. Classify the characteristics of a preceptor-resident interaction.

   CONFIDENCE: VC C N I VI ?

7. Negotiate the purpose of a precepting encounter with a resident.

   CONFIDENCE: VC C N I VI ?

8. Employ appropriate action for achieving the purpose of a given precepting encounter.

   CONFIDENCE: VC C N I VI ?

9. Define formative and summative evaluation.

   CONFIDENCE: VC C N I VI ?

10. Given an instructional objective, explain why certain evaluation methods are appropriate or inappropriate from the standpoint of validity, utility, and reliability.

    CONFIDENCE: VC C N I VI ?

11. Write an evaluation plan for an instructional unit explicitly identifying method(s) of formative evaluation for each objective.

    CONFIDENCE: VC C N I VI ?

12. Write an evaluation plan for an instructional unit explicitly identifying method(s) of summative evaluation for each objective.

    CONFIDENCE: VC C N I VI ?

13. Write an evaluation plan for an instructional unit explicitly identifying resources required for implementation.

    CONFIDENCE: VC C N I VI ?

14. Design an educational and personal support system for residents in a Family Medicine program.

    CONFIDENCE: VC C N I VI ?

15. List at least five benefits of conducting research in a primary care setting.

    CONFIDENCE: VC C N I VI ?

16. Evaluate a given data collection system, identifying its strengths and deficiencies.

    CONFIDENCE: VC C N I VI ?

17. Outline a plan for assuring quality control in a data system.

    CONFIDENCE: VC C N I VI ?

18. Formulate three research questions pertinent to one's own program.

    CONFIDENCE: VC C N I VI ?

19. Prepare a program budget for one year, differentiating between patient care and educational expenditures.

    CONFIDENCE: VC C N I VI ?

20. List developmental objectives for a residency program and develop a three-year projected budget which provides the financial resources to achieve those objectives.

    CONFIDENCE: VC C N I VI ?

21. Identify tasks currently being performed by physicians in a program which could be performed more cost-effectively by other personnel.

    CONFIDENCE: VC C N I VI ?

ASSESSMENT EXERCISE
Introduction

You are a member of the faculty of a Family Medicine Residency that is about to begin expanding from twelve to thirty-six residents. The Family Medicine Center is currently situated in a small medical office building; an expanded facility adequate to accommodate the larger group of providers is on the drawing board.

The residents see their own patients at the Family Medicine Center and rotate through various services at the local community hospital. Office practice experiences are also available to them on an elective basis.

The Center uses a problem-oriented medical record system. The Program is currently investigating the feasibility of computerizing this system for billing and research purposes.

The Center has a small but well-stocked library, tape recorders, and 35mm slide projection equipment. Additional, more sophisticated audiovisual hardware is planned for the new Center, but the budget will not allow for acquisition of such hardware for at least two more years. The community hospital also has a 16mm sound projector available for your use.

As part of the Program's evolution, the faculty decided it was time to prepare a curriculum document spelling out the Program's educational objectives. You have been selected to head the committee charged with this task.

One of your colleagues attended a workshop on educational methods, and he has developed some objectives for you to consider prior to the committee's first meeting. He asks you to critique each objective from the following perspectives:

1. Is the objective stated in performance-oriented terms?
2. Does the objective relate to the cognitive or skills domain?
3. What instructional method(s) would you consider suitable for addressing the objective in the family medicine center?
4. What method(s) of evaluating the residents would you consider suitable for addressing the objective in the family medicine center?

Instructions

1. Evaluate each objective *as it is written* (*not* as you might prefer that it be written).
2. For each statement, circle the number of the response(s) you would make to your colleague. Circle *only one* response if instructed to "Select the ONE BEST"; circle *one or more* if instructed to "Select AS MANY as appropriate."
3. Circle the corresponding number(s) on the answer sheet provided. Keep this copy of the assessment exercise. Turn in the answer sheet when you check in at the workshop.

NOTE: Since this exercise is intended to assess your ability to apply certain principles prior to workshop activities, please do not guess randomly. Answer only when you are reasonably confident about your response.

ASSESSMENT EXERCISE

OBJECTIVE A: TO TEACH THE LEARNER ABOUT COST DIFFERENCES IN MEDICATION.

a. This objective is stated in performance-oriented terms (Select ONLY ONE):
   1. Yes   2. No
b. This objective, as stated, relates PRIMARILY to the (Select ONLY ONE):
   1. Cognitive domain   2. Skills domain
c. Instructional methods both reasonable for this Program and suitable for this objective, as stated, include (Select AS MANY as appropriate):
   1. Discuss the topic in a precepting session.
   2. Give learner a list of comparative prices.
   3. Have learner spend two hours a week with hospital pharmacist.
   4. Refer learner to a recent issue of Medical Letter that gives price comparisons.

d. Methods of evaluating learners both reasonable for this Program and suitable for this objective, as stated, include (Select AS MANY as appropriate):
1. Observe learner's pattern of prescribing generic vs. brand names.
2. Give a written examination, including questions about the cost of medications.
3. During a precepting session, ask about differences in medication costs.
4. During a precepting session, ask if reducing medication costs is important in reducing health care costs.

OBJECTIVE B: THE LEARNER WILL KNOW HOW TO DEAL WITH AN ANGRY PATIENT.

a. This objective is stated in performance-oriented terms (Select ONLY ONE):
1. Yes   2. No
b. This objective, as stated, relates PRIMARILY to the (Select ONLY ONE):
1. Cognitive domain   2. Skills domain
c. Instructional methods both reasonable for this Program and suitable for this objective, as stated, include (Select AS MANY as appropriate):
1. Have learner view a videotape of a physician interviewing an angry patient.
2. Refer learner to a lecture on this topic being given by a psychiatrist.
3. Videotape the learner interviewing an actor portraying a hostile patient and discuss tape with learner.
4. Discuss the topic in a precepting session.
d. Methods of evaluating learners both reasonable for this Program and suitable for this objective, as stated, include (Select AS MANY as appropriate):
1. Give a written examination, including questions about dealing with angry patients.
2. Videotape learner interviewing an actor portraying a hostile patient and evaluate learner using a standard checklist.
3. During a precepting session, ask learner about ways of dealing with angry parents.
4. Ask patients how they feel about their interaction with the learner.

OBJECTIVE C: DESCRIBE THE FAMILY MEDICINE CENTER'S BILLING SYSTEM TO A LEARNER.

a. This objective is stated in performance-oriented terms (Select ONLY ONE):

1. Yes   2. No
b. This objective, as stated, relates PRIMARILY to the (Select ONLY ONE):
   1. Cognitive domain   2.   Skills domain
c. Instructional methods both reasonable for this Program and suitable for this objective, as stated, include (Select AS MANY as appropriate):
   1. Give a printed description of the system developed by the practice auditors.
   2. Discuss the topic in a precepting session.
   3. Have office manager discuss the system with learner.
   4. Refer learner to recent articles on comparative billing practices.
d. Methods of evaluating learners both reasonable for this Program and suitable for this objective, as stated, include (Select AS MANY as appropriate):
   1. Have learner write a description of the billing system he would prefer in future practice.
   2. During a precepting session, ask learner to describe the strengths of the Center's billing system.
   3. Give a written examination, including questions about the billing system.
   4. Have learner write a flowsheet showing the steps involved in the Center's billing process.

OBJECTIVE D: THE LEARNER LISTS IMMUNIZATIONS NEEDED BY AN EIGHTEEN-MONTH-OLD.
a. This objective is stated in performance-oriented terms (Select ONLY ONE):
   1. Yes   2. No
b. This objective, as stated, relates PRIMARILY to the (Select ONLY ONE):
   1. Cognitive domain   2.   Skills domain
c. Instructional methods both reasonable for this Program and suitable for this objective, as stated, include (Select AS MANY as appropriate):
   1. Refer learner to the "Red Book."
   2. Discuss the topic in a precepting session.
   3. Have learner audit charts of a sample of eighteen-month-olds in the Center's practice to determine if they are up-to-date.
   4. Have learner develop a bibliography of references empirically demonstrating the need for specific immunizations.
d. Methods of evaluating learners both reasonable for this Program and suitable for this objective, as stated, include (Select AS MANY as appropriate):
   1. During a precepting session, ask learner what immunizations are needed by an eighteen-month-old.

2. Audit charts of eighteen-month-olds seen by learner to determine if they are up-to-date in immunizations.
3. Give a written examination, including questions about immunizations.
4. Have learner write a short paper explaining the importance of proper immunization.

OBJECTIVE E: THE LEARNER DISTINGUISHES BETWEEN NORMAL AND ABNORMAL CHEST X-RAYS.

a. This objective is stated in performance-oriented terms (Select ONLY ONE):
   1. Yes   2. No
b. This objective, as stated, relates PRIMARILY to the (Select ONLY ONE):
   1. Cognitive domain   2. Skills domain
c. Instructional methods both reasonable for this Program and suitable for this objective, as stated, include (Select AS MANY as appropriate):
   1. Discuss the topic in a precepting session.
   2. Refer learner to a radiology textbook.
   3. Arrange for learner to read x-rays with radiologist at hospital.
   4. Have learner view a film describing principles of reading chest x-rays.
d. Methods of evaluating learners both reasonable for this Program and suitable for this objective, as stated, include (Select AS MANY as appropriate):
   1. Give a written examination, including questions about principles of reading x-rays.
   2. Ask learner to assess his own proficiency at interpreting x-rays.
   3. Ask learner to interpret a set of chest x-rays.
   4. During a precepting session, ask learner to describe the major findings that differentiate normal and abnormal chest x-rays.

FAMILY MEDICINE TEACHER TRAINING WORKSHOP
ASSESSMENT EXERCISE ANSWER SHEET

NAME:_____

OBJECTIVE	STATEMENT/RESPONSE			
A	a) 1 2	b) 1 2	c) 1 2 3 4	d) 1 2 3 4
B	a) 1 2	b) 1 2	c) 1 2 3 4	d) 1 2 3 4
C	a) 1 2	b) 1 2	c) 1 2 3 4	d) 1 2 3 4
D	a) 1 2	b) 1 2	c) 1 2 3 4	d) 1 2 3 4
E	a) 1 2	b) 1 2	c) 1 2 3 4	d) 1 2 3 4

FAMILY MEDICINE TEACHER TRAINING WORKSHOP
ASSESSMENT EXERCISE ANSWER SHEET

NAME:_____ANSWERS FOR PRETEST_____

OBJECTIVE	STATEMENT/RESPONSE			
A	a) 1 ②	b) ① 2	c) ①②3 ④	d) 1 ②③ 4
B	a) 1 ②	b) ① 2	c) 1 ② 3 ④	d) ① 2 ③ 4
C	a) 1 ②	b) ① 2	c) ①②③ 4	d) 1 ②③④
D	a) ① 2	b) ① 2	c) ①② 3 4	d) ① 2 ③ 4
E	a) ① 2	b) 1 ②	c) 1 2 ③ 4	d) 1 2 ③ 4

FAMILY MEDICINE TEACHER TRAINING WORKSHOP: PREPARATORY PROBLEMS (SIMULATION)

Introduction

These vignettes depict three situations of the "Why me?" variety that we will be discussing during the workshop. You may consult with others in resolving these problems. If you will be attending the workshop with another member of your faculty, the two of you may collaborate on a single set of resolutions. No-carbon-required worksheets are enclosed so you can give us a copy and keep one for yourself. Please type or print, unless your handwriting would win awards for clarity. But don't fret about scratching out words or making marginal notations. As long as it's reasonably decipherable, we won't be picky. A typed original with carbon or photocopy would be equally acceptable — the worksheets are included solely for your convenience and should be ignored if they interfere.

Remember that this is an experimental workshop. The Society of Teachers of Family Medicine will be evaluating all aspects of the workshop, with your opinions providing a key element of the evaluation. Please make note of your reactions to these materials as you work through them. If you still want to scream, we'll want to know.

PROBLEM 1: THE CHIEF RESIDENT'S COMPLAINT

You are attending a January meeting of your Family Medicine Residency Program's faculty at which the performance of the residents is being discussed.

The chief resident points out that at least three of the residents have been talking about leaving the Program. One said that he's

---

Developed by James A. Bobula, Ph.D., Stephen H. Gehlbach, M.D., and James T. Moore, M.D., Duke-Watts Family Medicine Program, Durham, North Carolina. Copyright © 1977 by the Duke-Watts Family Medicine Program. All rights reserved. Reprinted by permission.

been overwhelmed by the amount of work required and doesn't feel he has the knowledge base, clinical skills, or sheer energy to continue. Two commented that they are having doubts about careers in Family Medicine, even though they have been able to keep up with demands of the Program.

One of your faculty colleagues singles out four other residents who have received less than satisfactory evaluations on multiple occasions. In discussing these individuals, it becomes apparent that they are not seeking remedial assistance from any of you.

Problems like these have occurred before in the Program. On those occasions, one faculty member would volunteer to investigate a given resident's difficulties and help him or her resolve them. The chief resident expresses dissatisfaction with this patchwork approach. It is his impression that problems are occurring with greater frequency, that residents feel there's little interest in them unless they have trouble, and that the faculty should be able to anticipate and obviate at least some of these problems.

How would you respond to the chief resident? What plan would you devise to improve this situation?

PROBLEM 2: THE PRECEPTING DILEMMA

You are responsible for the precepting in your Family Medicine Residency Program's outpatient facility. You utilize full-time family medicine faculty and part-time private practitioners (family physicians, internists, surgeons, and pediatricians). Family medicine faculty precept three half days a week. Most of the private practitioners precept one half day a week, but a few visit on a monthly basis. To your knowledge, none of the preceptors has had formal training in instructional methods. Similarly the residents have not had formal training in how to use the preceptors effectively.

Recently you have received complaints from several of the residents about precepting. The most frequently voiced complaints include the following:

1. Due to the large number of patients seen, there is inadequate time to discuss problems with preceptors.
2. Some preceptors are unavailable when needed.
3. It is difficult for residents to get what they want from some

preceptors, i.e. preceptors have their own ideas about what they should be doing for the residents.

4. Some preceptors are insensitive in their consultant role and intrude into residents' relationships with their patients.

5. Some of the non-family medicine preceptors are unaware of basic aspects of ambulatory primary care, i.e. they are procedure- and hospital-oriented.

You have also received complaints from some of the preceptors, two of whom resigned recently. Their main complaint has been that they feel underutilized by the residents.

Attempting to put the residents' and preceptors' complaints in a realistic perspective, you proceeded to spend several half days at the Center observing the precepting as unobtrusively as possible. You have the following impressions:

1. Preceptors spend a lot of time sitting and waiting in the residents' lounge. It does appear that their skills are underutilized.

2. While residents do occasionally have periods that are very heavily scheduled with patients, it also appears that there are underscheduled periods when residents goof off at the Center or leave early.

3. At no time while you were at the Center did you see any evidence of a resident seeking the help of a preceptor and finding that none was available.

4. In trying to be unobtrusive in your observations, you did not listen in on any conversations between residents and preceptors. Thus you have no direct evidence of preceptors being insensitive to the residents or patients, or of preceptors recommending inappropriate care, although you are inclined to believe that these may well be problems with certain of your preceptors.

What steps would you now take toward resolving the problem of perceived deficiencies in precepting at the Family Medicine Center? Please be as specific as possible in describing each step.

PROBLEM 3: THE NEW DATA SYSTEM

You have been given the dubious honor of creating an automated data system for your Family Medicine Residency Program. You have read a great deal in the Family Medicine literature concerning various methods of collecting information, ranging from the "E" book to sophisticated computer systems. You have access to an outside computer firm which can handle your data processing, but you have been troubled by conflicting ideas on the best way of acquiring data. You tentatively decided to begin use of an "Encounter Form" which requires physicians to list the diagnostic problems encountered on each patient visit. However, problems are rapidly coming to your attention. Please respond to each of the following questions:

1. A nasty first year resident backed you into the corner with the question, "Why should I bother to fill out these forms? What's in it for me?" How do you answer this attack, and how can you get residents and faculty who are of this temperament to comply with your requests?

2. What steps can you take to insure the accuracy of the problems a physician lists on your form?

3. You have received several suggestions on who should be responsible for coding the listed problems for storage and processing by computer. Suggestions have ranged from hiring a special coder to requiring physicians to code their own forms. Who would you make responsible for coding, and how would you insure that coding is done reliably?

4. How would you insure sufficient numbers of encounter problems so that your data will be worthwhile?

CLINICAL SUPERVISION
(SIMULATION PROBLEM)
INSTRUCTIONS FOR SIMULATIONS

This is a *written simulation* of an instructional problem in undergraduate medical education. The problem can be resolved in a series of stages, each represented by a *section* in this simulation. Most sections will present new information and will ask you to choose among a number of options. Your task is to *choose the option(s) which best reflect(s) what you would actually do if you were* faced with that problem in the teaching you do. Even if the problem to be resolved is not appropriate to your present faculty role, select the option(s) which come closest to what you expect you would do if faced with that situation.

You may occasionally be presented with several options which all seem attractive, though you will be told to CHOOSE ONLY ONE. Choose the option you find to be closest to your characteristic instructional approach. You will likely have the opportunity to select from among the other options at a later point in the simulation.

To indicate which option you have selected, GENTLY rub once over the area just to the right of the asterisk (*), using the Latent Image Developer pen you have been given. A message will develop almost immediately. If the message is too light, gently rub the area a second time. Do this cautiously, however, as repeated rubbings can destroy the image. The end of the message is indicated by two asterisks (**). To test the system, answer this question:

Indicate whether you have used the latent image system before. (CHOOSE ONLY ONE):

1. I have used this system before.   *
2. I have never used this system before.   *

00

In working through this simulation, it is necessary for you to proceed from section to section precisely as directed by the instructions you

Developed by Hilliard Jason, M.D., Ed.D., Henry Slotnik, Ph.D., and R. Dale Lefever, Ph.D., Division of Faculty Development, Association of American Medical Colleges, Washington, D.C. All rights reserved. Copyright © 1976 by the Association of American Medical Colleges. Reprinted by permission. These materials are available from the National Center for Faculty Development, University of Miami School of Medicine, Miami, Florida.

receive within each section. *Develop only the option(s) you want.* The latent image response will (a) give you the information you requested, or (b) present you with the results of your action, or (c) direct you to the next appropriate section of the problem. Since this simulation was designed for use by a range of faculty members, there are more options, sections and information than any one person would use. This means you will be responding on only some of the pages, and that the number of sections you will use in managing the problem is likely to be different from the number used by others.

It will take approximately 15 minutes to complete most problems, although some may take less time. In any case, at the end you will see the words END OF PROBLEM in the message you develop. AT THAT POINT, PLEASE FOLLOW THE INSTRUCTION TO TURN TO THE QUESTIONNAIRE ON THE BACK COVER.

When you have finished reading these instructions, please begin the simulation.

Thank you.

"CLINICAL SUPERVISION"

You are a clinical preceptor responsible for supervising medical students toward the end of their "Introduction to Clinical Medicine" course, just prior to beginning their first clinical clerkship. In this course they have so far had general instruction in the conduct of history taking and physical examination. This morning you will work with Jim Scott, who will be doing his first complete new-patient workup. The other day you heard a passing comment from another faculty member that this student is "something of a dud." Your tasks today are: to evaluate his performance, to give him feedback, and to arrange whatever follow-up instruction you feel is appropriate. It is 9:00 a.m. and while the student is scheduled from 9–12, you can use as much or as little of the morning as you wish. You do want to find up to an hour to complete a project report that is due by noon. You and Jim greet each other and begin to plan the morning's activities.

You would now (CHOOSE ONLY ONE):

A1. Tell Jim to go ahead and examine the patient and   *
      to come to your office when he is ready to report
      his findings. You explain that you think that one
      hour should be all the time he will need.

A2. Tell Jim to go ahead and examine the patient and   *
      to call you if he runs into any problems. You
      explain that you think one hour should be all the
      time he will need.

A3. Ask Jim if he has any questions before he begins   *
      the workup.

A4. Engage Jim in a discussion of his prior   *
     experiences in this course.

A5. Ask Jim to begin the workup, explaining that you   *
     will sit in and observe what he does.

SECTION B

After working in your office on your report for a half hour, you reflect that you have not heard from Jim.

You would now (CHOOSE ONLY ONE):

B1. Walk over to the examining room, ask Jim to step   *
     out for a minute, and ask him how the workup is
     going.

B2. Join Jim in the examining room to observe the rest   *
     of the workup.

B3. Continue working until he calls you, or the hour is   *
     up, because you made it clear that he was to call if
     he was having trouble.

SECTION C

Jim gives a superficial overview of his experience to date in the "Introduction to Medicine" course, adding that he supposes he is ready to begin doing complete workups.

You would now (CHOOSE ONLY ONE):

C1. Ask him to begin the workup and to call you if he   *
     wants help.

C2. Ask him to tell you if he has run into any problems   *
     in working with patients.

C3. Ask him to begin the workup, indicating that you   *
     will sit in and observe what he does.

C4. Ask him if he is sure he understands what he is   *
     expected to do this morning.

C5. Ask him to begin his workup and to come to your   *
     office when he is done.

SECTION D

An hour has now passed since Jim began the workup, and he has not returned to your office.

You would now (CHOOSE ONLY ONE):

D1. Walk over to the examining room, ask Jim to step   *
     out for a minute, and ask how the workup is going.

D2. Go into the examining room, tell him that he   *
should bring the workup to an end within 20
minutes and that you would like to sit in on this
last part.

D3. Wait 20 minutes more and then call the clinic   *
nurse to interrupt the examination and have Jim
sent to your office.

SECTION E

Jim asks how long he should spend on the workup, and whether a
write-up will be necessary. You reply that one hour should be sufficient
and a verbal report is all that is expected.

You would now (CHOOSE ONLY ONE):

E1. Ask him to begin the workup and to call you if he   *
has any problems.

E2. Ask him if he is sure he understands what he is   *
expected to do this morning.

E3. Ask him to proceed with the workup and to come   *
to your office when he is done.

E4. Ask him to begin the workup, explaining that you   *
will sit in to observe what he does.

SECTION F

You accompany Jim to the examining room.

You would now (CHOOSE ONLY ONE):

F1. Introduce yourself and Jim to the patient and ask   *
Jim to begin the workup.

F2. Ask Jim to go ahead, and watch to see if he   *
introduces you and himself.

SECTION G

You watch Jim for 20 minutes during which time he concludes his
workup. In the process you take note of **(CHOOSE AS MANY AS ARE
APPROPRIATE IN ANY ORDER):**

G1. His method of asking questions.   *

G2. His elicitation of the "Chief Complaint" and   *
"History of Present Illness."

G3. His conduct of the review of systems.   *

G4. His approach to the social and family history.   *

G5. His mental status exam.   *

G6. His technique of palpation.   *

G7.   His technique of auscultation.   *

G8.   His technique of eliciting reflexes.   *

G9.   His method of giving instructions.   *

G10. His diagnostic formulation.   *

NOW GO TO SECTION N

SECTION H

Jim says that the patient has been uncooperative. She has been antagonistic during parts of the history and is now complaining in the early part of the physical exam.

You would now (CHOOSE ONLY ONE):

H1.   Tell him that he will just have to be more firm, to go   *
ahead and finish the workup, and to come to your
office when he is done.

H2.   Indicate that you will sit in on the rest of the exam   *
and try to help. You add that a patient's behavior
can be a reflection of the doctor's approach.

H3.   Indicate that this may be the result of something   *
he is doing and that you will watch the rest of the
workup to check that out.

SECTION J

Jim comes to your office, reports that he has finished the workup, and you indicate **(CHOOSE ONLY ONE):**

J1.   That completion of one's first full workup is a big   *
step. You ask him how it went, and to summarize
his findings.

J2.   That you would like him to summarize his main   *
findings from his workup, within no more than 20
minutes.

J3.   That he took a long time, and will now have to be   *
quicker in his summary, so that there will be time
for discussion. You ask him what he found.

SECTION L

On the basis of the information you now have about Jim's performance in the workup, you tell him **(CHOOSE ONLY ONE):**

L1.   That he is performing at a reasonable level given   *
his stage of training, and that with more
experience, he should continue to progress
satisfactorily.

L2. That you had heard he wasn't doing well in the   *
     clinical area, and you have little basis for changing
     that view. He is mechanical and rather insensitive
     and had better make an effort to improve in the
     future. You advise him to seek help.

L3. That you are generally satisfied with his   *
     performance this morning and wonder what else
     you can do to be helpful.

L4. That you are disappointed with his performance   *
     and that he will have to do better if he is to become
     a competent clinician. You ask how you can help.

SECTION M

You would now (CHOOSE ONLY ONE):

M1. Ask Jim to postpone his start of the workup,   *
     apologize to the patient, and explain that you don't
     want to miss any part of the examination.

M2. Ask Jim to continue with the workup, apologize to   *
     the patient, and indicate that you will get back as
     soon as you can.

SECTION N

   At the completion of the workup, you ask Jim to summarize his
findings and views. He indicates he's "glad it's over," and that she was a
"difficult patient." He then gives a fairly systematic, if mechanical,
review of his findings. On the basis of the information you now have you
tell him **(CHOOSE ONLY ONE):**

N1. That he is performing at a reasonable level given   *
     his stage of training, and that with more
     experience he should continue to progress
     satisfactorily. No immediate follow-up seems
     necessary.

N2. That you were impressed with his thoroughness.   *
     He did a nice physical exam, is clearly trying hard,
     and if he is a little more understanding with
     patients, he should become a good clinician. No
     immediate follow-up seems necessary.

N3. That you had heard he wasn't doing well in the   *
     clinical area, and you have little basis for changing
     that view. He is mechanical and rather insensitive
     and had better make an effort to improve in the
     future. You advise him to seek help.

N4. That you were satisfied with how he managed   *

parts of the physical and parts of the history. But before he can get to be a good clinician, there are some issues that need attention. You provide some specific suggestions and conclude by scheduling an appointment for another meeting.

N5. That if you are to be helpful, you've got to come * right to the point and say that he really treated that patient quite badly. He was insensitive and harsh at times, and must be quite insecure to be arguing with a patient the way he did. You ask how you can help with these problems.

SECTION O

Jim responds that he has found several of his patients in the "Introduction to Medicine" course to be quite uncooperative.

You would now (CHOOSE ONLY ONE):

O1. Indicate that this is a common problem and that he * should begin his workup and come to your office when done.

O2. Suggest that it may well have been partly his fault * and that you are expecting him to do better today.

O3. Indicate that many beginners feel this way. Ask * him to begin the workup and to call you if he wants help.

O4. Indicate that it is important to try to understand * why that happens, and that you will be sitting in with him today so that you can help if that problem emerges with this patient.

O5. Indicate that this can be a focus of attention this * morning; but that before he begins his workup you want to be sure he understands what is expected of him.

SECTION P

You rejoin Jim and the patient in the examining room and observe the full workup. In the process you take note of **(CHOOSE AS MANY AS ARE APPROPRIATE IN ANY ORDER):**

P1. His method of asking questions. *

P2. His elicitation of the "Chief Complaint" and * "History of Present Illness."

P3. His conduct of the review of systems. *

P4. His approach to the social and family history. *

P5. His mental status exam. *

P6.   His technique of palpation.   *
P7.   His technique of auscultation.   *
P8.   His technique of eliciting reflexes.   *
P9.   His method of giving instructions.   *
P10. His diagnostic formulation.   *

NOW GO TO SECTION N   *

SECTION R

Jim indicates that he was planning to follow the outline of a complete workup that was handed out earlier in the course, but would appreciate your guidance. You emphasize that you will be looking at **(INDICATE WHETHER YOU WOULD INCLUDE OR EXCLUDE EACH ITEM BELOW):**

NOTE: AN X WILL APPEAR
TO RECORD YOUR
DECISION ON EACH ITEM.

		Would Include	Would Not Include
R1.	His method of asking questions.	*	*
R2.	His elicitation of the "Chief Complaint" and "History of Present Illness."	*	*
R3.	His conduct of the review of systems.	*	*
R4.	His approach to the social and family history.	*	*
R5.	His mental status exam.	*	*
R6.	His technique of palpation.	*	*
R7.	His technique of auscultation.	*	*
R8.	His technique of eliciting reflexes.	*	*
R9.	His method of giving instructions.	*	*
R10.	His diagnostic formulation.	*	*

In view of the above, you would now (CHOOSE ONLY ONE):

R11. Ask him to begin the workup and to call you if he   *
      has any problems.
R12. Ask him to begin the workup and to come to your   *
      office when he is done.
R13. Ask him to begin the workup, explaining that you   *
      will sit in to observe what he does.

SECTION S

You rejoin Jim and the patient, apologize for missing the first 10 minutes, and observe the remainder of the workup. In the process you take note of **(CHOOSE AS MANY AS ARE APPROPRIATE IN ANY ORDER):**

S1.   His method of asking questions.   *

S2.   His elicitation of the "Chief Complaint" and   *
       "History of Present Illness."

S3.   His conduct of the review of systems.   *

S4.   His approach to the social and family history.   *

S5.   His mental status exam.   *

S6.   His technique of palpation.   *

S7.   His technique of auscultation.   *

S8.   His technique of eliciting reflexes.   *

S9.   His method of giving instructions.   *

S10. His diagnostic formulation.   *

NOW GO TO SECTION N

FACULTY DEVELOPMENT
NEEDS ASSESSMENT*

I.D._____

Introduction: The purpose of this form is to determine areas in which faculty members feel a need to improve their abilities. The information you provide here will be used to design future faculty development workshops and seminars for our department. Individual responses will be confidential. Please return the completed form no later than_____ using the enclosed envelope. At the same time but separate from your completed form, please mail the enclosed card. This card informs me that you have sent in your form and I will not need to send you reminders.

Before beginning the survey, please place in the upper right corner of this page an ID number or name that you will be able to recall several months from now. In order to assess the effectiveness of our faculty development efforts, I need to be able to compare your responses now to future information you give me. I will be able to do this, and still keep your data confidential by matching IDs on various instruments used over the next year. So that you don't forget your ID, you may wish to use such things as your social security number, birthdate, telephone number, former dog tag number, mother's maiden name, or pet's name.

This is a four-part instrument. Part I asks for demographic data; Part II asks about faculty skills in teaching, research, and general administration; Part III asks about faculty skills in advanced administration; and Part IV asks about your satisfaction as a faculty member. Detailed instructions precede each section when necessary.

The results of this survey will be reported at a faculty meeting. Thank you in advance for your co-operation.

PLEASE DO NOT BEGIN UNLESS YOU HAVE READ THE INTRODUCTIONS AND PLACED AN ID IN UPPER RIGHT HAND CORNER.

PART ONE: DEMOGRAPHIC DATA

Instructions: Please complete the following questions related to your background.

1. Your age (check one):
   ____under 31   ____31-40   ____41-50   ____51-60   ____61-70   ____above 70
2. Your faculty rank (check one):
   ____Professor ____Associate Professor ____Assistant Professor ____Instructor ____Research Fellow
   ____Administrative Fellow   ____Clinical Professor   ____Unsure   ____Other (identify)
3. Administrative responsibilities (check all that apply):
   ____Head or associate head of Department or Unit   ____Committee Chair
   ____Coordinator of special area (e.g. communications group, PHS, etc.)   ____ Other (identify)
4. Highest degree obtained_____ Date received_____
5. Total faculty experience (any and all institutions)
   ____(number of years) — Solely volunteer   ____(number of years) — Paid part-time
   ____(number of years) — Paid full-time
6. Please list any Faculty Development Workshops/Seminars in which you have participated within the last 5 years.

Workshop/Seminar Title	*Sponsor*	*# Hours*	*Emphasis*

---

* Developed by Carole J. Bland, Ph.D., Department of Family Practice and Community Health, University of Minnesota, Minneapolis, Minnesota.

7. Professional specialty (e.g. family physician, clinical psychologist)

8. What percent of your time is spent as a *paid* faculty member of the Department of Family Practice and Community Health? _____%.

9. Please indicate the approximate number of *hours* you spend in an average *week* doing each of the following activities.

Activity	*Number of Hours Spent*
One-to-one precepting	_____
Formal classroom lecture	_____
Rounds	_____
Other instruction	_____
Research/writing professional articles	_____
Administration	_____
Committees	_____
Patient care	_____
Continuing education	_____
Other (please give examples) _____	_____
_____	_____

10. Please indicate what *percent* of your Family Practice time you spend at each of the following places:

_____ University Family Practice Department (e.g. meeting or seminar rooms, your office, non-clinic setting)

_____ University hospital/clinic

_____ Affiliated hospitals/clinics (e.g., St. John's, Methodist)

_____ County hospitals/clinics

_____ Duluth hospitals/clinics

_____ Private practice/satellite clinic (e.g. Nokomis, Ebenezer, PHS. clinic, etc.)

_____ Other (identify)_____

_____ " " _____

_____ " " _____

*100%** TOTAL

*Please note that this column should add up to 100% even if you are a part-time faculty member.

11. How interested are you in participating in seminars and workshops designed to increase teaching, research, and administration skills? (CHECK ONE)

_____ *Very interested;* would take great pains to rearrange my schedule to attend workshops/seminars in most or all areas.

_____ *Somewhat interested;* would attend if it were convenient.

_____ *Not at all interested;* would not attend.

PART TWO: TEACHING, RESEARCH, AND GENERAL ADMINISTRATIVE SKILLS

Instructions: The following is a list of research, teaching, and general administrative skills. Below each skill are statements which describe someone who needs a great deal of training in the skill (1) to someone who needs no further training (5). A description is also provided of the person whose ability is between these two extremes. For each skill, please indicate where you fall on the continuum by circling the number (1, 2, 3, 4, or 5) that best describes you. Also, please indicate what you think your skill level *SHOULD* be as a faculty member of the Department of Family Practice and Community Health. Don't be concerned if you are not at the highest ability level on many skills. No one will be a "5" in all areas. Also, it is possible that on some skills, you will think you need have only minimum abilities to function comfortably and effectively in your faculty position.

TEACHING SKILLS

1. TEACHING-LEARNING THEORY

A. Have little understanding of the *theories of learning* (e.g. behavior modification, discovery learning, rational model).

Am familiar with basic *learning theories* and could apply them in a teaching situation after some review.

Am well versed in *learning theory* and can effectively apply the tenets to a teaching situation.

1	2	3	4	5

My skill level *IS:*

1	2	3	4	5

I think my skill level *SHOULD* be:

2. NEEDS ASSESSMENT

A. Have little understanding of how to determine ability of incoming students through *needs assessment.*

Could construct one after some review.

Am proficient at constructing and using the results of *needs assessment.*

1	2	3	4	5

My skill level *IS:*

1	2	3	4	5

I think my skill level *SHOULD* be:

3. GOAL STATEMENTS/EDUCATIONAL OBJECTIVES

A. Have little understanding of what a *goal statement* is.

Could write *goal statements* after some review.

Could write succinct *goal statements* for instruction based on student needs.

1	2	3	4	5

My skill level *IS:*

1	2	3	4	5

I think my skill level *SHOULD* be:

B. Have little understanding of what an *objective* is, the purpose of objectives or how to formulate them from goal statements.

Have an understanding of what an *objective* is and could derive specific objectives from goal statements with some preparation.

Can easily state desired instructional goals and specific outcomes *(objectives)* in measurable behavioral terms.

1	2	3	4	5

My skill level *IS:*

1	2	3	4	5

I think my skill level *SHOULD* be:

4. TEACHING AIDS

A. Once my instructional goals and objectives are set, I have little idea as to what teaching aids (books, videotapes, guest lecturers, etc.) are *already available* to help meet the objectives.

I can locate *already available* teaching aids, but only with a lot of effort.

I have a complete and continually updated list of available *ready-made* materials and am able to make effective use of teaching aids at my disposal to meet goals and objectives.

	1		2		3		4		5

My skill level *IS:*

	1		2		3		4		5

I think my skill level *SHOULD* be:

B. Would find it very difficult to *prepare* materials to help learners accomplish objectives.

Can *develop* some materials but need assistance.

Can easily *develop* various materials that aid both teaching and learning.

	1		2		3		4		5

My skill level *IS.*

	1		2		3		4		5

I think my skill level *SHOULD* be:

5. TEACHING STRATEGIES

A. Have little idea of the factors to consider in *selecting* among various teaching strategies (e.g. lecture, demonstration, microteaching, small group discussion).

I am fairly comfortable in matching a teaching strategy (i.e. am familiar with the factors to consider) to the topic and students I need to teach.

I can easily weight the indications and contraindications as well as my preference and logistic considerations in *selecting* among various teaching strategies.

	1		2		3		4		5

My skill level *IS:*

	1		2		3		4		5

I think my skill level *SHOULD* be:

B. Although I have been with students, I am uncertain as to how to effectively *use* various *teaching strategies.*

Could effectively *use* alternative *strategies* after some review.

Am completely aware of and facile in *using* alternative *teaching strategies.*

	1		2		3		4		5

My skill level *IS:*

	1		2		3		4		5

I think my skill level *SHOULD* be:

C. Within teaching strategies, I have little idea of the effects of various *communication techniques* and cannot *use* them (e.g. questioning, feedback, establishment of rapport).

Have a good understanding of the effects of these *techniques* but probably don't *use* them as consistently as I should.

Have a complete understanding of the principles of various *communication techniques* and effectively *use* each one.

	1		2		3		4		5

My skill level *IS:*

	1		2		3		4		5

I think my skill level *SHOULD* be:

6 MANAGE THE TEACHING EXPERIENCE

A. Have difficulty *organizing* my teaching into sequentially logical units and alloting the appropriate amount of time to each unit.

Have some idea of sequence and an approximate amount of time to leave for each unit.

Have no difficulty in *organizing* materials into logical sequences or in estimating the amount of time that should be alloted for each unit.

1	2	3	4	5

My skill level *IS:*

1	2	3	4	5

I think my skill level *SHOULD* be:

B. Once in the teaching situation, I seem to *present* things too fast, too slow and/or out of sequence and I cannot seem to readjust properly.

Presentation is sometimes difficult to follow in that the pace is off or my order is confused. However, initial feedback from the learners serves to help me adjust my presentation and I'm okay after that.

Am usually right on target in terms of pacing, sequencing and adjusting my materials.

1	2	3	4	5

My skill level *IS:*

1	2	3	4	5

I think my skill level *SHOULD* be:

7 EVALUATION TECHNIQUES AND TOOLS

A. Have little idea of how to begin to *construct* an evaluation instrument (e.g. questionnaire, test, interview schedule).

Could make a good stab at *constructing* an instrument and could probably come up with a usable one.

Am proficient at *devising* all types of evaluation techniques and know which ones are appropriate for a given situation.

1	2	3	4	5

My skill level *IS:*

1	2	3	4	5

I think my skill level *SHOULD* be:

B. Have little idea of what types of *analyses* to perform on evaluation data or how to go about doing them.

Can locate someone to help me, and with effort, can explain my *analyses* needs to them.

Am proficient at choosing the type of *analyses* I need and can perform them myself or easily find someone who can.

1	2	3	4	5

My skill level *IS:*

1	2	3	4	5

I think my skill level *SHOULD* be:

C. Once I have the results of the evaluation, I am uncertain as to how to *interpret* them.

With some help, I can *translate* the results of the evaluation data into changes in my instruction and/or recommendations for students.

Am able to *interpret* evaluation data and do such things as assess student performance and alter instruction, if necessary.

1	2	3	4	5

My skill level *IS:*

1	2	3	4	5

I think my skill level *SHOULD* be:

8 CONSULTANTS

A. Am uncertain as to where to begin to look for a *consultant* to assist me with teaching problems (e.g. curriculum design, improving teaching strategies, evaluation, etc.).

Could find a *consultant* and elicit information from him/her with some effort on my part.

Have a running list of *specialists* in the field of education from whom I could obtain immediate assistance.

1	2	3	4	5

My skill level *IS:*

1	2	3	4	5

I think my skill level *SHOULD* be:

9 MANAGE ADVISEES: CHECK IF NOT APPLICABLE ☐

A. Would have difficulty recognizing my *advisees* if I passed them on the street.

Able to maintain routine contact with each of my *advisees*.

Actively seek to maintain contact with my *advisees* and keep current on their problems and progress.

1	2	3	4	5

My skill level *IS:*

1	2	3	4	5

I think my skill level *SHOULD* be:

10. DISCIPLINE OF MEDICAL EDUCATION

A. Have little awareness of what journals and *literature* exist in medical education and/or such articles are difficult to read and utilize.

Am familiar with medical education journals and *literature* and, with effort, can extract the important findings.

Am well aware of journals and *literature,* can quickly and efficiently assimilate information from technical articles, and can critically analyze and identify flaws in research methodology.

1	2	3	4	5

My skill level *IS:*

1	2	3	4	5

I think my skill level *SHOULD* be:

B. Am uncertain as to how to find out about *nonliterature* resources available to me (e.g. conferences, CME courses, conventions, etc.).

Am usually aware of *nonliterature* resources and am able to make limited use of them.

Have a good system for keeping informed of *such resources* and make frequent use of a wide variety of them.

1	2	3	4	5

My skill level *IS:*

1	2	3	4	5

I think my skill level *SHOULD* be:

11. TEACHING REWARDS

A. Have difficulty identifying *rewards* associated with my teaching.

Can identify a few *rewards* and have some general plans for obtaining them (e.g. opportunity to share knowledge, positive interpersonal interchange, promotion).

Can idenfity many *rewards* associated with my teaching role and can utilize effective means for obtaining them.

| 1 | 2 | 3 | 4 | 5 |

My skill level *IS:*

| 1 | 2 | 3 | 4 | 5 |

I think my skill level *SHOULD* be:

OTHER TEACHING SKILLS

Please write here any teaching skills you would like to increase that were not included above.

RESEARCH SKILLS

1. RESEARCH QUESTIONS

A. Am uncertain as to how to identify a topic or problem which could be researched.

Could formulate general research questions arising out of my own interests and experiences.

Can formulate a specific, feasible research question, and if appropriate, put it in the form of a statistical hypothesis.

| 1 | 2 | 3 | 4 | 5 |

My skill level *IS:*

| 1 | 2 | 3 | 4 | 5 |

I think my skill level *SHOULD* be:

2. CONDUCTING RESEARCH

A. Have little familiarity with various research *designs* (e.g. experimental, quasi-experimental, time series).

Have some idea of different *designs.*

Can identify several different research *designs* and discuss the strengths and weaknesses of each.

| 1 | 2 | 3 | 4 | 5 |

My skill level *IS:*

| 1 | 2 | 3 | 4 | 5 |

I think my skill level *SHOULD* be:

B. Know little about how to select an optimal *sample size* or *sampling strategy* (e.g. random, stratified, matched, etc.).

Have some idea of different *sampling strategies* and factors to consider in determining *size.*

For a given situation, can identify the appropriate *sampling strategy* and *sample size.*

| 1 | 2 | 3 | 4 | 5 |

My skill level *IS:*

| 1 | 2 | 3 | 4 | 5 |

I think my skill level *SHOULD* be:

C. Would have difficulty identifying or selecting among various *data collection* methods.

Have some idea of the problems and strategies of *data collection* (e.g. chart audit, observation, interviews, questionnaire, counts).

Can describe alternative methods of *data collection* and the strengths and weaknesses of each (e.g. response rates problems, cost and time requirements, possible biases).

1	2	3	4	5

My skill level *IS:*

1	2	3	4	5

I think my skill level *SHOULD* be:

D. Have little familiarity with ways of *analyzing* and *interpreting data* (statistical tests, content analysis, graphic analysis).

Am familiar with various types of analyses but would need to review criteria for selection, performance and interpretation of results.

Am proficient at selecting the appropriate analyses and computing and interpreting the results.

1	2	3	4	5

My skill level *IS:*

1	2	3	4	5

I think my skill level *SHOULD* be:

3. RESEARCH CONSULTANTS

A. Have little idea as to where to start *looking* for help with a research problem.

Have some idea of the kinds of specialists I need and where to *locate* them.

I know exactly *who* to consult at each point in the research process.

1	2	3	4	5

My skill level *IS:*

1	2	3	4	5

I think my skill level *SHOULD* be:

B. Can sense when there is a problem with a study but would find it difficult to *communicate* it to a research design consultant.

Have some idea of the types of questions to *ask* a research design consultant.

Know exactly how to *communicate* to a design consultant to get quick and efficient responses.

1	2	3	4	5

My skill level *IS:*

1	2	3	4	5

I think my skill level *SHOULD* be:

4. SCHOLARLY WRITING

A. Have few of the necessary skills (e.g. ability to be concise, clear, make transitions, be grammatically correct) to *write* an article, proposal, position paper, etc.

Could produce a good paper with a considerable amount of editing.

Possess highly developed writing *skills* (e.g. ability to be concise, clear, make transitions, be grammatically correct) and could produce a good paper with little or no editing.

1	2	3	4	5

My skill level *IS:*

1	2	3	4	5

I think my skill level *SHOULD* be:

5. RESEARCH PRESENTATIONS

A. Have difficulty *organizing* a topic for presentation at conferences, rounds, meetings, conventions, etc.	Can do an adequate job of *organizing* a topic.	Am highly skillful at *organizing* a topic for easy understanding.
1	2	3	4	5

My skill level *IS:*

| 1 | 2 | 3 | 4 | 5 |

I think my skill level *SHOULD* be:

B. Have difficulty in *orally* communicating a topic to others.	I can *speak* with much rehearsal but I wouldn't call it dynamic or charismatic.	Can *orally* present a topic in a dynamic, interesting, and effective manner.
1	2	3	4	5

My skill level *IS:*

| 1 | 2 | 3 | 4 | 5 |

I think my skill level *SHOULD* be:

6. RESEARCH DISCUSSIONS

A. Have found little opportunity to talk on a one-to-one basis with anyone about my research interests.	Know a few individuals (e.g. colleagues) with whom I can discuss my research interests.	Have developed a network of colleagues with whom I regularly initiate discussion about our research.
1	2	3	4	5

My skill level *IS:*

| 1 | 2 | 3 | 4 | 5 |

I think my skill level *SHOULD* be:

7. DISCIPLINE OF RESEARCH INTEREST

A. Have little awareness of what journals or *literature* exist relevant to my research interests and/or such articles are difficult to read and utilize.	Am familiar with relevant *materials* and can extract the important findings.	Know exactly where to find *materials,* can quickly and efficiently assimilate information from technical articles, and can critically analyze and identify flaws in research methodology.
1	2	3	4	5

My skill level *IS:*

| 1 | 2 | 3 | 4 | 5 |

I think my skill level *SHOULD* be:

B. Am unclear as to how to find out about or use *nonliterature* resources in my area of research interest (e.g. conferences, CME courses, conventions, etc.).	Am usually aware of and make limited use of *such resources.*	Have a good system for keeping informed of and productively use a variety of *such resources.*
1	2	3	4	5

My skill level *IS:*

| 1 | 2 | 3 | 4 | 5 |

I think my skill level *SHOULD* be:

8. RESEARCH REWARDS

A. Have difficulty identifying *rewards* associated with my research.	Can identify a few *rewards* and have some general plan for obtaining them (e.g. opportunity to share findings or synthesis in area of knowledge, publication, promotion).	Can identify many *rewards* associated with my research and can utilize effective means for obtaining them.

| 1 | 2 | 3 | 4 | 5 |

My skill level *IS:*

| 1 | 2 | 3 | 4 | 5 |

I think my skill level *SHOULD* be:

OTHER RESEARCH SKILLS

Please write here any research skills you would like to increase that were not included above.

GENERAL ADMINISTRATIVE SKILLS

1. POLICY MAKING

A. Have little idea how policies are *established* within the department.	Could describe several ways policies are *established* within the department.	Could describe several ways policies are *established* within the department; would know who to talk to (which committee) if I wanted to influence a certain policy.

| 1 | 2 | 3 | 4 | 5 |

My skill level *IS:*

| 1 | 2 | 3 | 4 | 5 |

I think my skill level *SHOULD* be:

B. Generally cannot determine how my own *administrative tasks* relate to an overall policy or when a policy affects me directly.	Usually know how my own *administrative tasks* relate to an overall policy and my role in implementing a policy; could describe the administrative functions of the administrative heads in the department.	Clearly know how my own *administrative tasks* relate to an overall policy and my role in implementing a policy; could describe the administrative functions of nearly all members of the department.

| 1 | 2 | 3 | 4 | 5 |

My skill level *IS:*

| 1 | 2 | 3 | 4 | 5 |

I think my skill level *SHOULD* be:

2. PERSONAL MANAGEMENT SKILLS

A. Haven't given much thought to *management skills* or style necessary to interact effectively with others such as office staff, student assistants, and co-workers.

Have thought about and could describe my *management style.*

Could describe my *management style* as it relates to theories or principles of management; can adapt my style to the needs of the work environment.

1	2	3	4	5

My skill level *IS:*

1	2	3	4	5

I think my skill level *SHOULD* be:

3. INFORMATION FLOW

A. Have difficulty in identifying the administrative s*ources of information* when I have a question.

Have an adequate understanding of the administrative *sources of information* for most of my information needs, and generally know how to respond to information requests.

Can i d e n t i f y administrative *sources* and systematically obtain required information; organize relevant information efficiently; and respond to information requests and deadlines.

1	2	3	4	5

My skill level *IS:*

1	2	3	4	5

I think my skill level *SHOULD* be:

4. GROUP FUNCTIONING

A. Experience difficulty in most aspects of *group functioning* (includes being clear about my and others' responsibilities, participating fully, taking advantage of others' expertise, and following through on assigned tasks).

Experience difficulty in one or two aspects of *group participation* listed.

Am highly skillful in all aspects of *group participation.*

1	2	3	4	5

My skill level *IS:*

1	2	3	4	5

I think my skill level *SHOULD* be:

5. DISCIPLINE OF EDUCATIONAL ADMINISTRATION

A. Have little awareness of what journals or *literature* exist in educational administration and/or such articles are difficult to read and utilize.

Am familiar with relevant educational administration *materials* and can extract the important findings.

Know exactly where to find *materials,* can quickly and efficiently assimilate information from technical articles, can critically analyze and can identify flaws in research methodology.

1	2	3	4	5

My skill level *IS:*

1	2	3	4	5

I think my skill level *SHOULD* be:

B. Am uncertain as to how to find out about *nonliterature* resources on educational administration (e.g. conferences, CME courses, conventions, etc.).

Am usually aware of and make limited use of *such resources.*

Have a good system for keeping informed of and productively use a variety of *such resources.*

| 1 | 2 | 3 | 4 | 5 |

My skill level *IS:*

| 1 | 2 | 3 | 4 | 5 |

I think my skill level *SHOULD* be:

6. ADMINISTRATIVE REWARDS

A. Have difficulty identifying *rewards* associated with my administrative responsibilities.

Can identify a few *rewards* (e.g. having a voice in policy making, securing the information I need, taking care of administrative details quickly) and have some general plans for obtaining them.

Can identify many *rewards* associated with my administrative role and can utilize effective means for obtaining them.

| 1 | 2 | 3 | 4 | 5 |

My skill level *IS:*

| 1 | 2 | 3 | 4 | 5 |

I think my skill level *SHOULD* be:

OTHER GENERAL ADMINISTRATIVE SKILLS

Please write here any administrative skills you would like to increase that were not included above.

PART THREE: ADVANCED ADMINISTRATIVE SKILLS

PLEASE READ INSTRUCTIONS BEFORE YOU PROCEED

Instructions: This section addresses advanced administrative skills most likely needed by faculty members with greater administrative responsibilities. Examples of such faculty include the Department Head, Unit Directors, directors of grant projects, and directors of special programs or groups such as Program in Human Sexuality, Rural Physician Associate Program, Communications, and Educational Research and Development Group. If you are one of these faculty members, please indicate *your ability* by circling the appropriate number on the continuum for each of the items. Also, indicate the ability level you think you *SHOULD* possess. If you do *not* have advanced administrative responsibilities, please use the second continuum only and indicate the level of responsibility you think administrative faculty *SHOULD* possess.

ADVANCED ADMINISTRATIVE SKILLS

1. LIAISON

A. Have thought little about ways to systematically convey expectations of *higher levels* (e.g. university, medical school, department, faculty) to my own level. Lack a strategy for assuring that an accurate image of higher level is conveyed to my level.

Have an adequate system to convey the more important expectations of *high levels* to own level; avoid major problems in communication; neither enhance nor detract from image of higher levels.

Consistently understand and systematically convey expectations of *higher levels* to own level; actively promote a positive image of higher levels.

1	2	3	4	5

My skill level *IS:*

1	2	3	4	5

I think my skill level *SHOULD* be:

B. Have thought little about ways to systematically communicate *my levels's* needs (e.g. residency unit, special program or group, faculty, department, medical school) to higher levels, or actively promote image of own level.

Can communicate needs of *my level* to higher level at least on important issues; and neither enhance nor detract from image of my own level.

Have excellent understanding of *my own level's* needs and can systematically communicate them to higher levels; actively promote positive image of own level.

1	2	3	4	5

My skill level *IS:*

1	2	3	4	5

I think my skill level *SHOULD* be:

2. FACULTY/STAFF RELATIONSHIPS

A. Ignore *conflict,* or have few effective ways to intervene; may respond more to certain groups than others.

Have ability to generally resolve or reduce *conflict* before it becomes a crisis; consciously strive to treat faculty/staff fairly.

Able to maintain faculty/staff morale by an ability to effectively respond to or prevent *conflict,* show sensitivity to faculty/staff needs and treat all faculty/staff members fairly.

1	2	3	4	5

My skill level *IS-*

1	2	3	4	5

I think my skill level *SHOULD* be:

3. FACULTY/STAFF DEVELOPMENT

A. Have occasionally, but not systematically supported *faculty/staff development* efforts.

Have some plans for *faculty/staff development* and identifying rewards for self-starters.

Have established plans for promoting faculty/staff abilities and systematically encourage and reward *faculty/staff development.*

1	2	3	4	5

My skill level *IS:*

1	2	3	4	5

I think my skill level *SHOULD* be:

4. FACULTY/STAFF EVALUATION

A. Can contribute little to the planning of an *evaluation system* or not able to use effectively one already established.

Able to use an already established *system* but not able to contribute to its improvement.

Able to guide the development of *evaluation* and to systematically use evaluation results.

| 1 | 2 | 3 | 4 | 5 |

My skill level *IS:*

| 1 | 2 | 3 | 4 | 5 |

I think my skill level *SHOULD* be:

5. UNIT/DEPARTMENTAL GROUP ADMINISTRATION

A. Do not always *operate* the department/unit/group according to a particular organizational plan.

Able to *operate* the department/unit/group from an organizational plan but it is not always explicit.

Able to *run* the department/unit/group by sound organizational principles taking into account long-range planning in terms of growth, change, financial needs, etc.

| 1 | 2 | 3 | 4 | 5 |

My skill level *IS:*

| 1 | 2 | 3 | 4 | 5 |

I think my skill level *SHOULD* be:

6. FACULTY/STAFF QUALITY BALANCE

A. Unable to *maintain* a department/unit/group with quality faculty/staff.

Able to *ensure* adequate faculty/staff by adequate interest in recruiting.

Able to *ensure* quality faculty/staff by careful recruiting and by encouraging productive and rewarding activities with the department/unit/group.

| 1 | 2 | 3 | 4 | 5 |

My skill level *IS:*

| 1 | 2 | 3 | 4 | 5 |

I think my skill level *SHOULD* be:

B. Unable to maintain an appropriate *balance* of specialties, level of training, personality, etc.

Able to maintain a decent *balance* of types of faculty.

Able to maintain just the right *balance* of types of faculty to ensure a well-functioning department/unit/group.

| 1 | 2 | 3 | 4 | 5 |

My skill level *IS:*

| 1 | 2 | 3 | 4 | 5 |

I think my skill level *SHOULD* be:

OTHER ADVANCED ADMINISTRATIVE SKILLS

Please write here any administrative skills you would like to increase that were not included above.

PART FOUR: SATISFACTION

Instructions: Please indicate how strongly you agree or disagree with each of the following statements.
(circle one)

	Strongly Disagree	Disagree	Agree	Strongly Agree
1. A. I feel that I am an effective *teacher*.	SD	D	A	SA
B. I feel that I am an effective *researcher*.	SD	D	A	SA
C. I feel that I am an effective *administrator*.	SD	D	A	SA
2. A. I feel appreciated as a *teacher*.	SD	D	A	SA
B. I feel appreciated as a *researcher*.	SD	D	A	SA
C. I feel appreciated as an *administrator*.	SD	D	A	SA
3. A. I feel that being a *teacher* is personally rewarding.	SD	D	A	SA
B. I feel that being a *researcher* is personally rewarding.	SD	D	A	SA
C. I feel that being an *administrator* is personally rewarding.	SD	D	A	SA
4. A. I feel comfortable in my role as a *teacher*.	SD	D	A	SA
B. I feel comfortable in my role as a *researcher*.	SD	D	A	SA
C. I feel comfortable in my role as an *administrator*.	SD	D	A	SA
5. I feel my contributions as a teacher, researcher, and administrator are as valuable as those I could make by practicing full time in my field.	SD	D	A	SA

Again, thank you for completing this survey. Please return it using the enclosed envelope. Don't forget to mail, separate from your form, your card saying you've mailed your completed survey.

Appendix VII

WORKSHOP BUDGET

Workshop Title _____

Workshop Dates _____

Workshop Location _____

Sponsor _____

Funding Source(s) _____

(e.g., tuition, sponsor, funding agency)

Date Budget Prepared _____

Budget Approvals: Sponsor _____

Funding Agency (if necessary) _____

INCOME

I. SOURCES

	Totals	Category Total	Rationale
A. Sponsor (Institution/Organization)	$____		
B. Grants or Contracts			
C. Participants		$____	
TOTAL INCOME (Same as Category Total)		$____	

EXPENSES

I. PERSONNEL

	name	*time*	*rate*	Subtotals	Totals	Category Total	Rationale
A. Planners, Teachers			$____	$____	$____		
B. Secretaries, Assistants							
C. Consultants, Guest Speakers						$____	

Prepared by Patricia Pihak, Executive Director, Minnesota Association for Children with Learning Disabilities, St. Paul, Minnesota.

II. TRAVEL

				Subtotals	Totals	Category Total	Rationale
A. Transportation	*mode*	*# travelers*	*avg. cost* $				
1. Planners, Teachers				$___			
2. Secretaries, Assistants				___			
3. Consultants, Guest Speakers				___			
4. Participants				___	$___		
B. Room and Board	*# rooms*	*# days*	*cost/day avg. R & B*				
1. Planners, Teachers				___			
2. Secretaries, Assistants				___			
3. Consultants, Guest Speakers				___			
4. Participants				___	___	$___	

III. FACILITY

				Subtotals	Totals	Category Total	Rationale
A. Meeting rooms	*# rooms*	*# days*	*cost/day*				
1. Rental				$___			
2. Set-ups (special seating, etc.)				___	$___		
B. Food & Refreshments	*date/type*	*# served*	*cost (incl. tip)*				
1. Catered meals (B,L,D)	/			___			
	/			___			
	/			___			
2. Refreshments	/			___	___		
				___			
C. Entertainment, Special Programs	*event*	*# persons*	*cost/person*				
				___	___	$___	

	Subtotals	Totals	Category Total	Rationale

IV. ADMINISTRATIVE

A. Supplies
   1. Expendable Items (pens, flip charts, tablets, etc.)
   2. Educational Materials (textbooks, workbooks, etc.)
B. Equipment (rental or purchase)

   #   *cost/piece*

   1. 35 mm projectors
   2. Screens
   3. Video playback monitors
   4. Cameras
   5. Tape players
   6. Overhead projectors
   7. Chalkboards
   8. Mikes
   9. Lecterns

C. Telephone
   item   *cost/piece*

D. Graphics and Reproduction
   item   *cost/piece*

E. Postage and Freight

F. Other
   TOTAL EXPENSES (Sum of Category Total)

DIFFERENCE BETWEEN INCOME AND EXPENSE

I.   Total Income $
     less
II. Total Expenses $
III. Difference (Net Profit Net Loss, Break Even) $

WHAT TO EXPECT WHEN APPLYING FOR EXTERNAL FUNDS

The following briefly describes what you can expect when applying to external sources. In describing what to expect when applying to an external source, the following three assumptions are made:

1. The purpose of your workshop is compatible with the agency's guidelines and priorities.
2. Your workshop proposal, including all the items listed above, is in its penultimate form.
3. You can submit the proposal in the required form by the agency's deadline.

Given these assumptions, outlined below is what you can expect when soliciting funds from the federal government or a foundation.

FEDERAL AGENCIES

Allow six to eight months from the time that you submit the proposal until the day you receive the good or bad news. Briefly, in general what happens to your proposal during this time period is as follows, although variations occur:

- Proposal is received, logged into computer, given an identification number.
- Proposal is checked for necessary signatures. If any are missing, expect a delay.
- Proposal is given to selected members of the peer review committee.
- Some agencies conduct a site visit.
- Committee members who reviewed your proposal make recommendations to the total peer committee.
- The peer committee determines which proposals should be considered for funding and assigns them a priority score.

Written by Maureen Moo-Dodge, Grant Coordinator, Department of Family Practice and Community Health, University of Minnesota, Minneapolis, Minnesota.

- Their recommendations and priority score are referred to a national advisory committee that authorizes monies to as many projects as the allocated funds can cover. In other words, a high priority score doesn't necessarily mean that you receive dollars.

NATIONAL FOUNDATIONS

Allow four to six months when negotiating with a national foundation. The sequence of events will probably include the following:

- Review by staff member of your preliminary proposal (four to six page letter).
- Notification within thirty days of foundation's interest in your proposal.
- Request by foundation for complete proposal, if interested.
- Possible site visit by foundation representatives before final decision is made.
- Foundation accepts or rejects proposal. If accepted, funding is guaranteed.

LOCAL FOUNDATIONS

Allow two to four months for the application review process to be completed. One big advantage in dealing with local foundations is the possibility of personal contact. Meeting foundation staff members and lining up their support can improve your prospects. Your first contact with a local foundation will probably be a letter of inquiry, which is most effective if it is actually a two to five page miniproposal. Here's what to expect next:

- Staff review of your miniproposal or letter of inquiry.
- Request for personal interview from foundation. (You may want to initiate this request by a phone call.)
- Request by foundation for full proposal, if interested.
- Review of full proposal by foundation staff.
- Possible site visit by foundation representatives before final decision is made.
- Foundation accepts or rejects proposal; acceptance assures funding.

Appendix IX

FINANCIAL REPORT (Periodic or Final)

Workshop Title _____ Sponsor _____

Workshop Dates _____ Funding Sources _____

Workshop Location _____ Date of Report _____

INCOME

I. SOURCES

	Budgeted Amount	Amount to Date (ATD)	Difference (Budget minus ATD)	Rationale
A. Sponsor (Institution/Organization)	$_____	$_____	$_____	
B. Grants or Contracts	_____	_____	_____	
C. Participants	_____	_____	_____	
TOTAL INCOME	$_____	$_____	$_____	

EXPENSES

I. PERSONNEL

	Budgeted Amount	Amount to Date (ATD)	Difference (Budget minus ATD)	Rationale
A. Planners, Teachers	$_____	$_____	$_____	
B. Secretaries, Assistants	_____	_____	_____	
C. Consultants, Guest Speakers	_____	_____	_____	

II. TRAVEL

A. Transportation				
1. Planners, Teachers	$_____	$_____	$_____	
2. Secretaries, Assistants	_____	_____	_____	
3. Consultants, Guest Speakers	_____	_____	_____	
4. Participants	_____	_____	_____	

Prepared by Patricia Plhak, Executive Director, Minnesota Association for Children with Learning Disabilities, St. Paul, Minnesota.

143

	Budgeted Amount	Amount to Date (ATD)	Difference (Budget minus ATD)	Rationale
B. Room and Board	$_____	$_____	$_____	
1. Planners, Teachers	_____	_____	_____	
2. Secretaries, Assistants	_____	_____	_____	
3. Consultants, Guest Speakers	_____	_____	_____	
4. Participants	_____	_____	_____	
III. FACILITY				
A. Meeting rooms	$_____	$_____	$_____	
1. Rental	_____	_____	_____	
2. Set-ups (special seating, etc.)	_____	_____	_____	
B. Food and Refreshments				
1. Catered meals (B, L, D)	_____	_____	_____	
2. Refreshments	_____	_____	_____	
C. Entertainment, special programs				
IV. ADMINISTRATIVE				
A. Supplies	$_____	$_____	$_____	
1. Expendable items (pens, flip charts, tablets, etc.)	_____	_____	_____	
2. Educational materials (textbooks, workbooks, etc.)	_____	_____	_____	
B. Equipment				
1. 35mm projectors	_____	_____	_____	
2. Screens	_____	_____	_____	
3. Video playback monitors	_____	_____	_____	
4. Cameras	_____	_____	_____	
5. Tape players	_____	_____	_____	
6. Overhead projectors	_____	_____	_____	

	Budgeted Amount	Amount to Date (ATD)	Difference (Budget minus ATD)	Rationale
7. Chalkboards	$	$	$	
8. Mikes				
9. Lecterns				
C. Data Processing				
D. Telephone				
E. Graphics and Reproduction				
F. Postage and Freight				
TOTAL EXPENSES	$	$	$	

DIFFERENCE BETWEEN INCOME AND EXPENSES

I. Total Income $ _____

   less

II. Total Expenses $ _____

III. Difference (Net Profit, Net Loss, Break Even) $ _____

FACULTY ACTIVITIES RATING

INSTRUCTIONS

Identification
Number:

Listed below are three sets of statements which describe various activities related to Faculty of Family Practice Programs. For items 1-21 indicate your feeling about the importance of each activity and how knowledgeable you feel about each. Use the scales shown below.

Importance   V = Very important
Rating: S = Somewhat important
               N = Not important

Knowledge   4. Very knowledgeable
Rating: 3. Somewhat knowledgeable
             2. Somewhat unknowledgeable
             1. Very unknowledgeable

(circle one)   *(circle one)*

V	*S*	*N*			*VK*	*SK*	*SU*	*VU*
V	*S*	*N*	*1.*	*Assess the needs of students in my area of expertise.*	*4*	*3*	*2*	*1*
V	*S*	*N*	*2.*	*Write curriculum goal statements.*	*4*	*3*	*2*	*1*
V	*S*	*N*	*3.*	*Locate and use resources needed for curriculum design.*	*4*	*3*	*2*	*1*
V	*S*	*N*	*4.*	*Write instructional objectives based on goal statements.*	*4*	*3*	*2*	*1*
V	*S*	*N*	*5.*	*Devise strategies and allocate resources to help students meet learning objectives.*	*4*	*3*	*2*	*1*
V	*S*	*N*	*6.*	*Exhibit skill in using communicative techniques which aid resident learning*	*4*	*3*	*2*	*1*

Developed by Robert A. Reineke, Ph.D. and Wayne W. Welch, Ph.D. for the Society of Teachers of Family Medicine, Kansas City, Missouri.

			i.e., persuasion, rapport, timing and pacing.					
V	S	N	7. *Devise and use tests of resident abilities.*		4	3	2	1
V	S	N	8. *Utilize certain statistical and experimental design methods for course planning and student evaluations.*		4	3	2	1
V	S	N	9. *Use evaluation information (feedback) to implement changes in teaching strategies.*		4	3	2	1
V	S	N	10. *Know and use the organizational structure including lines of authority and the informal power structure (including delegating authority when appropriate).*		4	3	2	1
V	S	N	11. *Identify administrative information sources and systematically obtain required information.*		4	3	2	1
V	S	N	12. *Maintain a convenient file of useful information.*		4	3	2	1
V	S	N	13. *Respond to organizational information requests and deadlines.*		4	3	2	1
V	S	N	14. *Function as a committee member and make use of committee expertise to accomplish your objectives.*		4	3	2	1
V	S	N	15. *Utilize resources (especially colleagues) within your department to upgrade skills in less familiar areas of family practice disciplines.*		4	3	2	1
V	S	N	16. *Practice in the various disciplines of family practice.*		4	3	2	1
V	S	N	17. *Maintain contact with developments within the field of family practice and in related fields, e.g., critically review research in professional literature.*		4	3	2	1

V　　S　　N　　18. Formulate research ideas in acceptable research design formats including use of design consultants when necessary.　　　4　3　2　1

V　　S　　N　　19. Write journal articles, position papers and grant proposals.　　　4　3　2　1

V　　S　　N　　20. Prepare and deliver interesting and informative presentations appropriate for conferences, rounds, meetings and conventions.　　　4　3　2　1

V　　S　　N　　21. Provide information in both formal and informal one-to-one situations (e.g., an advisor, a colleague and a subordinate).　　　4　3　2　1

Items 22-32 refer to personal skills and objectives. Respond to these items as above. Note that the scale on the right refers to a self-assessment of your strength or limitation for each item.

4. *Personal strength*
3. *Above average*
2. *Below average*
1. *Personal limitation*

V　　S　　N　　22. Establish personal rapport with residents.　　　4　3　2　1

V　　S　　N　　23. Hone teaching skills so as to be entertaining and brief as well as informative.　　　4　3　2　1

V　　S　　N　　24. Give each resident personal help in learning when needed.　　　4　3　2　1

V　　S　　N　　25. Share skills and teaching experiences with colleagues.　　　4　3　2　1

V　　S　　N　　26. Meet formal requirements for promotion and official recognition as a preceptor.　　　4　3　2　1

V　　S　　N　　27. Set personal teaching objectives and assess your accomplishments against them.　　　4　3　2　1

V　　S　　N　　28. Offer administrative assistance to colleagues.　　　4　3　2　1

V	S	N	29. Seek credit for your accomplishments and the accomplishments of others, when deserved.	4	3	2	1
V	S	N	30. Participate in the social milieu of the organization.	4	3	2	1
V	S	N	31. Take personal pride in and contribute to the recognition of the field of family practice.	4	3	2	1
V	S	N	32. Seek colleagues whose recognition and appreciation is valued.	4	3	2	1

Items 33-36 ask how you feel about your role as a faculty member. Respond to these items as above (their importance) and indicate the extent to which you agree or disagree with each.

AA = Strongly agree   A = Agree   D = Disagree   DD = Strongly Disagree

V	S	N	33. I am very comfortable in my role as a faculty member.	AA	A	D	DD
V	S	N	34. I feel appreciated as a faculty member.	AA	A	D	DD
V	S	N	35. My contribution to Family Practice Medicine would be greater as a practitioner than as a teacher.	AA	A	D	DD
V	S	N	36. Teaching Family Medicine is a personally rewarding experience.	AA	A	D	DD

PARTICIPANT QUESTIONNAIRE

SPRING PRESESSION ON RESEARCH

GENERAL INSTRUCTIONS: The purpose of this questionnaire is to gather four types of information: your perception as to your preworkshop and postworkshop ability to do specific research activities; your opinions as to the suitability and quality of the workshop as a whole as well as its subparts and some descriptive data about yourself. This information will be used to aid the development of similar workshops in the future. Your candid response to all items is appreciated. Thank you for your assistance.

PARTICIPANT DESCRIPTION

Instructions: Please fill in the following spaces related to your background and institution.

1. Position/title (e.g., director of residency program, head of behavioral science division, clinic preceptor):

    _____

2. Highest Degree_____ Date Received_____

3. Faculty designation (check one):
    ___Full Professor   ___Instructor
    ___Associate Professor   ___Research Assistant
    ___Assistant Professor   ___Research or Teaching Assistant
    ___Clinical Faculty   ___Other (specify)_____

4. Your past faculty experience: _____(years)—Solely volunteer
                                    _____(years)—Paid—part-time
                                    _____(years)—Paid—full-time

5. What percent of time is spent as a paid faculty member? (check one)
    ___100%   ___50-99%   ___10-49%   ___Under 10%

6. What percent of your faculty time is spent in research?_____

7. With what type of institution do you have your primary administrative

From *Evaluation Report: STFM Research Workshop*, Coronado, California, May 4-6, 1978. Workshop coordinated by Stephen Gehlbach, M.D. Report prepared by Carole J. Bland, Ph.D.

relationship? This is often the institution whose name appears on your paycheck. (check one)

___University   ___Federal agency
___Community Hospital   ___Military
___County Hospital   ___Other (specify)_____

8.   How far did you travel to attend this workshop (one way)?_____miles

Research Activities Rating

Listed below are two sets of statements which describe various research activities of a faculty member in Family Practice Programs. First, read items 1–17 and on the left side indicate how able you were to do each *before* you attended this workshop. Reread items 1–17 and on the right side indicate how able you are to do each *after* having attended this workshop. Use the scales shown below.

ABILITY RATING: 4. Very able (VA)   2. Somewhat not able (SNA)
                     3. Somewhat able (SA)   1. Not at all able (NA)

| My ability on this skill *Before* Workshop | | | | | | My ability on this skill *After* Workshop | | | |
VA	SA	SNA	NA			VA	SA	SNA	NA
4	3	2	1	1.	Developing general research questions from my own practice experience.	4	3	2	1
4	3	2	1	2.	Listing the variables that need to be measured to answer a research question, citing a method for measuring each variable, listing the resources required, and estimating the feasibility of measuring each variable.	4	3	2	1
4	3	2	1	3.	Restating a general research question as a specific, feasible question, i.e., refined research question.	4	3	2	1
4	3	2	1	4.	Identifying 3 basic study designs (descriptive, explanatory, experimental) and citing a function and limitation of each.	4	3	2	1
4	3	2	1	5.	Defining and suggesting ways to deal with 4 major problem areas in the structural design of studies, i.e., time/history, experiment/observation, selection and regression.	4	3	2	1
4	3	2	1	6.	Outlining a data collection system appropriate to my own practice.	4	3	2	1

4 3 2 1   7. Identifying local resources for aiding   4 3 2 1
              research.

4 3 2 1   8. Distinguishing between a sample and   4 3 2 1
              a population or a universe.

4 3 2 1   9. Detecting ambiguities and/or inconsis-   4 3 2 1
              tencies between samples and the popu-
              lation they purport to represent.

4 3 2 1   10. Distinguishing appropriate from inappro-   4 3 2 1
              priate uses of tests of statistical signifi-
              cance (this does not include selection
              of particular tests of significance).

4 3 2 1   11. Discussing, in general terms, the effects   4 3 2 1
              of increasing or decreasing sample size
              on interpretation of results.

4 3 2 1   12. Discussing the considerations which   4 3 2 1
              are germane to the determination of
              sample size.

4 3 2 1   13. Consulting knowledgeably with a statis-   4 3 2 1
              tician in order to determine a reason-
              able sample size.

4 3 2 1   14. Using fictitious tables and graphs to dis-   4 3 2 1
              play likely results of my studies.

             15. Critiquing the presentations of others
              with respect to three items:

4 3 2 1   a. finding ambiguities in research ques-   4 3 2 1
                 tions

4 3 2 1   b. finding multiple interpretations of re-   4 3 2 1
                 sults

4 3 2 1   c. finding omissions of data which limit   4 3 2 1
                 the interpretations

4 3 2 1   16. Explicitly stating my expectations of   4 3 2 1
              study results.

             17. Discussing the value of the literature re-
              view as a means to:

4 3 2 1   a. begin with more informed expecta-   4 3 2 1
                 tions

4 3 2 1   b. identify additional variables to con-   4 3 2 1
                 sider

4 3 2 1   c. identify other possibilities for design,   4 3 2 1
                 analysis, or display of data

Items 18-21 ask how you feel about your research role as a faculty
member. First, respond to these items by indicating the extent to which

you agreed or disagreed with each *before* the workshop. Then reread the items and indicate your present feelings *after* the workshop.

AA = Strongly Agree A = Agree D = Disagree DD = Strongly Disagree

My feelings Before Workshop		My feelings After Workshop
AA A D DD	18. I am very comfortable in my research role as a faculty member.	AA A D DD
AA A D DD	19. I feel appreciated as a faculty member who does research.	AA A D DD
AA A D DD	20. My contribution to Family Practice Medicine would be greater as a practitioner than as a researcher.	AA A D DD
AA A D DD	21. Conducting research in Family Medicine is a personally rewarding experience.	AA A D DD

Quality and Suitability of Workshop Subparts

Instructions: Please rate each workshop subpart using the following categories:

KEY:	*Value of Topic*	*Level of Content Presented*	*Quality of Presentation*
	(How valuable was this topic to you)	(Consider practicality of information presented)	(Consider speaking expertise, organization and visual aids)
	EV = Extremely Valuable	TE = Too Esoteric	E = Excellent
	VV = Very Valuable	SE = Slightly Esoteric	VG = Very Good
	V = Valuable	U = Useful	G = Good
	SV = Slightly Valuable	SB = Slightly Basic	F = Fair
	NV = Not Valuable	TB = Too Basic	P = Poor

	Value of Topic (Circle one)	*Level of Content Presented* (Circle one)	*Quality of Presentation* (Circle one)
FIRST DAY			
8:40- 8:50 "The Big Picture"—Steve Gehlbach	EV VV V SV NV	TE SE U SB TB	E VG G F P
9:45-10:00 "Formulating Research Questions"— David Marsland	EV VV V SV NV	TE SE U SB TB	E VG G F P
10:40-11:15 "Refining Questions"— George Parkerson	EV VV V SV NV	TE SE U SB TB	E VG G F P

1:45- 2:15 "Creating Research Design"— Steve Gehlbach	EV VV V SV NV	TE SE U SB TB	E VG G F P

SECOND DAY

8:45-10:00 "Anticipating Results"— Michael Gordon	EV VV V SV NV	TE SE U SB TB	E VG G F P
10:15-11:30 "Data Collection"—David Marsland	EV VV V SV NV	TE SE U SB TB	E VG G F P
1:10- 2:00 "Sampling"—Michael Gordon	EV VV V SV NV	TE SE U SB TB	E VG G F P

THIRD DAY

8:45- 9:15 "Turning on Residents"— Gehlbach and Gordon	EV VV V SV NV	TE SE U SB TB	E VG G F P
2:00- 2:40 "Identifying and Utilizing Resources and Wrap Up"—Gehlbach and Gordon	EV VV V SV NV	TE SE U SB TB	E VG G F P

*Considering all three days, how valuable was each of
the following:*

Individual Work Sessions	EV VV V SV NV
Small Group Work Sessions	EV VV V SV NV
Presentations on Group Projects	EV VV V SV NV
Critiques of Individual's Projects	EV VV V SV NV

General Workshop Reactions

Instructions: Participants at previous workshops of this type have made the following statements about their workshop experiences. Please express your degree of agreement or disagreement with each statement.

DD = Strongly Disagree; D = Disagree; U = Uncertain; A = Agree; AA = Strongly Agree

(Circle one)

1. "Most of what was covered the past few days will *not* be very helpful when I get back home." DD D U A AA

2. "The staff at this workshop seemed very competent." DD D U A AA

3. "I *didn't* like the style of this workshop." DD D U A AA

4. "I feel good about this workshop experience." DD D U A AA

5. "I wish I had stayed home." DD D U A AA

6. "I feel better about being a researcher in family medicine because of this workshop." DD D U A AA

7. "This workshop should be made available to all faculty in family medicine." DD D U A AA

8. "I would recommend this workshop to a colleague." DD D U A AA

9. "This workshop was one of the best I've ever attended." DD D U A AA

10. "Too much time was spent on *nonproductive* activities." DD D U A AA

11. "I think I will be a better faculty member because of this course." DD D U A AA

12. "The things I learned here will be valuable to the rest of my colleagues back home." DD D U A AA

13. "As a result of this workshop I will be able to implement the project I brought with me." DD D U A AA

14. "Much of the workshop was a waste of my time." DD D U A AA

15. "The fancy research stuff sounds good, but it just *won't* work for me." DD D U A AA

16. "Most of the presenters were poorly prepared." DD D U A AA

17. "I wish the preworkshop materials had been better." DD D U A AA

18. "This workshop accomplished most of the objectives I listed the first day." DD D U A AA

Instructions: Please rate each of the following aspects of the workshop on the 9-point scale by circling the number that best describes your feelings.

1. FACILITIES/SETTING 9   8   7   6   5   4   3   2   1
Excellent.   Adequate.   Poor.

2. OBJECTIVES 9   8   7   6   5   4   3   2   1
Clearly stated and useful to me.   Generally clear and occasionally helpful.   Not apparent or inappropriate.

3. STAFF 9   8   7   6   5   4   3   2   1
Highly competent and interesting.   Average ability, some limitations.   Ill prepared and uninteresting.

4. FELLOW PARTICIPANTS 9   8   7   6   5   4   3   2   1
A congenial group which enhanced this experience.   Were neither a positive nor negative factor for this workshop.   Hard to relate to, detracted from this experience.

5. ACTIVITIES 9   8   7   6   5   4   3   2   1
Very appropriate for workshop goals, rewarding.   Most okay, a few inappropriate or of limited value.   Not very helpful, uninteresting, vague.

6. COST	9	8	7	6	5	4	3	2	1
	Well worth the money, a real bargain.			Moderately reasonable.			A waste of time and money.		

7. OUTCOMES	9	8	7	6	5	4	3	2	1
	I feel I learned a great deal.			I've learned a few new things.			Nothing new learned of any value.		

8. ORGANIZATION	9	8	7	6	5	4	3	2	1
	Very organized.			Adequate organization.			Unorganized.		

Recommendations

1. What changes would you suggest in the workshop to improve the experience for persons like yourself?

2. What components / features would you especially want retained in future workshops?

3. Additional Comments:

PARTICIPANT FEEDBACK

I. WORKSHOP ELEMENTS

1. OBJECTIVES
1) Are workshop objectives clear? _____
2) Do they meet your needs? _____
3) Suggested improvements

2. MATERIALS
1) Do materials fit the objectives? _____
2) Are they meeting your needs? _____
3) Suggested improvements

3. STAFF
1) Is staff working well as a team? _____
2) Consistent or contradictory? _____
3) Suggested improvements

4. CONSULTANTS
1) Are outside resource people adding to learning? _____
2) List any who are not. _____
3) Suggested improvements

5. PARTICIPANTS
1) How well is staff relating to your needs (content or personal)? _____
_____
2) Do you feel a need to become better acquainted with other participants? _____
_____
3) Suggested improvements

6. STRUCTURE
1) Are group size and composition helpful to learning? _____
2) Are physical arrangements for group work appropriate? _____
3) Suggested improvements

Reprinted from *Planning, Conducting, and Evaluating Workshops — Workshop Staff Packet* by Larry Nolan Davis by permission of Learning Concepts. Copyright © 1974 by Larry Nolan Davis.

7. AIDS

1) Are learning aids appropriate? _____
2) Supplies adequate? _____
3) Suggested improvements

8. FACILITY

1) Problems
2) Suggested improvements

9. ACCOMMODATIONS
(if applicable)

1) Problems
2) Suggested improvements

10. FOOD AND REFRESHMENTS

1) Problems
2) Suggested improvements

11. DATES

1) Will you need to leave early? _____ When? _____
2) If activities need to be extended, are you available? _____
3) How long?

12. TRAVEL

1) Problems in getting to or from workshop?
2) Suggested improvements

13. FUTURE NEEDS

1) Have you discovered additional learning needs? _____
2) What?

14. TIME

1) Is pace of learning activities appropriate? _____
2) Suggested improvements

15. METHODS

1) Which type of learning activities worked best?
2) Which encountered problems?
3) Suggestions

16. ENERGY/ATTENTION

1) Are more/fewer breaks needed? _____
2) Was your energy or attention lower at certain times? _____
3) When? _____4) Why? _____

17. CLIMATE

1) Is the overall climate or mood of this workshop supportive of your learning? _____

2) Suggestions

II. GROUP OBSERVATIONS

Use the following guide to help pinpoint any problems you noticed
while participating in small group activities.

1. Did group(s) seem to favor certain attitudes or behaviors over others? Did this cause problems? Describe.

2. In getting its work done, did group overlook individual feelings or contributions? Did group attention to individual concerns keep it from accomplishing its task? Describe.

3. Did members share effectively in group workload? Did certain members do all the work, or always do same work? Describe.

4. Did group develop its own leadership? Was leadership too authoritarian, too loose, or appropriate? Describe.

5. Did the behavior of certain individuals block the group learning? Describe (you may or may not use names).

6. Did the group(s) have trouble in reaching decisions? Describe.

7. Were there problems in the degree of cooperation/competition between groups? Describe.

8. Others.

FACILITY SURVEY

REQUIREMENTS

Workshop: Other requirements

No. Participants _____ No. Meeting Rooms _____

Size   Times

_____   _____

_____   _____

_____   _____

SURVEY DATA

Facility Name   Address

Contact   Telephone

AVAILABILITY

		No. Meeting	
Dates	Times	Rooms	Acceptable
_____	_____	_____	( )
_____	_____	_____	( )
_____	_____	_____	( )

| | | | Yes | No |
| **COSTS** $_____ | Tips? _____ | Affordable | ( ) | ( ) |

ACCESSIBILITY

PARKING (Free or fee?)

OVERALL QUALITY

OTHER COMMENTS

EQUIPMENT   Available (✓)

| Chalkboards ( ) | Projectors ( ) | P.A. system ( ) | Water pitchers ( ) |
| Easels ( ) | _____ ( ) | Mikes ( ) | Glasses ( ) |

Reprinted from *Planning, Conducting, and Evaluating Workshops—Workshop Staff Packet* by Larry Nolan Davis by permission of Learning Concepts. Copyright © 1974 by Larry Nolan Davis.

Screen	( )	_____	( )	Adequate tables	( )	Ash trays	( )
Lecterns	( )	Tape player	( )	Adequate chairs	( )	Cups	( )
_____	( )	_____	( )	_____	( )	_____	( )
_____	( )	_____	( )	_____	( )	_____	( )

REFRESHMENT NEEDS   Check (✓) where appropriate

Catered / Cost (incl. tips)

Coffee	( )	$_____	Cokes	( )	$_____
Water	( )	$_____	Ice	( )	$_____
Tea	( )	$_____	Booze	( )	$_____
_____	( )	$_____	_____	( )	$_____
_____	( )	$_____	_____	( )	$_____

We must provide

Coffee	( )	Sugar	( )	Ice	( )
Water	( )	Cream	( )	Booze	( )
Tea	( )	Cups	( )	Mixers	( )
Cokes	( )	Glasses	( )	_____	( )
_____	( )	_____	( )	_____	( )

FOOD   Catered

	Caterer	Costs (incl. tips)
B	_____	$_____
L	_____	$_____
D	_____	$_____

Not Catered

	Restaurants in Area		Est. Cost to Participant
Convenience	_____	B	$_____
Speed	_____	L	$_____
Variety	_____	D	$_____
Quality	_____		

ASSORTED NEEDS

Telephones _____		Copy machine _____
Messages _____		Restroom convenience _____
Others _____		_____
_____		Cleanup arrangements _____

ACCOMMODATIONS

REQUIREMENTS

Workshop:

   No. Participants___ No. Rooms___

Type	No.	Price range
Single / 1 bd.	___	$_____
Double / 1 bd.	___	$_____
Double / 2 bd.	___	$_____
Suites	___	$_____

Other requirements

SURVEY DATA

Establishment   Address

Contact   Telephone

DATES (Possible dates for sufficient rooms) _____ _____

_____ _____

ROOMS

Types	No. available	Price range	No. reserved
Single / 1 bd.	_____	$_____ to $_____	_____
Double / 1 bd.	_____	$_____ to $_____	_____
Double / 2 bd.	_____	$_____ to $_____	_____
Suites	_____	$_____ to $_____	_____

Proximity To Meeting (describe)

  No. rooms   Proximity

_____   _____

_____   _____

_____   _____

_____   _____

Rooms Generally

  Acceptable (✓)   Unacceptable (x)

Appearance	( )	Bed comfort	( )	Telephones	( )
Restrooms	( )	Closet space	( )	TV	( )
Cleanliness	( )	Noise insulation	( )	Reading chair	( )
Tem. control	( )	Lighting	( )	Desk	( )

Reservation Policy

Late Check-out Policy

OTHER
Convenience of:

Entertainment_____

Recreation_____

Food_____

Liquor laws_____

Special Attractions

Description	Dates
_____	_____
_____	_____
_____	_____

Services (describe)

Laundry_____

Medical_____

Messages_____

MEETING ROOMS   Acceptable (✓)   Unacceptable (x)

No. or name   Size   Seating Capacity   Appearance

1._____ _____ ( ) _____ ( ) _____ ( )
Convenience to other rooms _____ ( )
Entrance/exit adequate_____ ( )   Noise level_____ ( )
Heating/air cond.   ( ) Elec. outlets   ( )   Lighting   ( )
Ventilation/smoke   ( ) Windows   ( )   Carpets   ( )
Darkening drapes   ( ) Room height   ( )
Room flexibility_____ ( )
Furniture movability_____ ( )

MEETING ROOM 1   Acceptable (✓)   Unacceptable (x)

No. or name   Size   Seating Capacity   Appearance

_____ _____ ( ) _____ ( ) _____ ( )
Convenience to other rooms _____ ( )
Entrance/exit adequate_____ ( )   Noise level_____ ( )
Heating/air cond.   ( ) Elec. outlets   ( )   Lighting   ( )
Ventilation/smoke   ( ) Windows   ( )   Carpets   ( )
Darkening drapes   ( ) Room height   ( )
Room flexibility_____ ( )
Furniture movability_____ ( )

MEETING ROOM 2   Acceptable (✓)   Unacceptable (x)
                                              Seating
No. or name   Size   Capacity   Appearance
_____   _____ ( ) _____ ( ) _____ ( )
Convenience to other rooms _____ ( )
Entrance / exit adequate_____ ( )   Noise level_____ ( )
Heating / air cond.   ( ) Elec. outlets   ( ) Lighting   ( )
Ventilation / smoke   ( ) Windows   ( ) Carpets   ( )
Darkening drapes   ( ) Room height   ( )
Room flexibility_____ ( )
Furniture movability_____ ( )

MEETING ROOM 3   Acceptable (✓)   Unacceptable (x)
                                              Seating
No. or name   Size   Capacity   Appearance
_____   _____ ( ) _____ ( ) _____ ( )
Convenience to other rooms _____ ( )
Entrance / exit adequate_____ ( )   Noise level_____ ( )
Heating / air cond.   ( ) Elec. outlets   ( ) Lighting   ( )
Ventilation / smoke   ( ) Windows   ( ) Carpets   ( )
Darkening drapes   ( ) Room height   ( )
Room flexibility_____ ( )
Furniture movability_____ ( )

MEETING ROOM 4   Acceptable (✓)   Unacceptable (x)
                                              Seating
No. or name   Size   Capacity   Appearance
_____   _____ ( ) _____ ( ) _____ ( )
Convenience to other rooms _____ ( )
Entrance / exit adequate_____ ( )   Noise level_____ ( )
Heating / air cond.   ( ) Elec. outlets   ( ) Lighting   ( )
Ventilation / smoke   ( ) Windows   ( ) Carpets   ( )
Darkening drapes   ( ) Room height   ( )
Room flexibility_____ ( )
Furniture movability_____ ( )

Appendix XIV

A DIRECTORY OF CONSULTANTS
IN FACULTY DEVELOPMENT

CURRICULUM

A. Higher Education

William Bergquist, Ph.D.
Consultant
1217 Campus Drive
Berkeley, CA 94708
(415) 845-2299

Lawrence Demarest, Ph.D.
Director of Educational
    Development and Evaluation
St. Mary's Junior College
2500 South 6th Street
Minneapolis, MN 55454
(612) 332-5521

Robert M. Diamond, Ph.D.
Assistant Vice Chancellor
Center for Instructional
    Development
Syracuse University
115 College Place
Syracuse, NY 13210
(315) 423-4571

Paul L. Dressel, Ph.D.
Professor of University
    Research
Michigan State University

Room 331
Hannah Administration
    Building
East Lansing, MI 48824
(517) 355-6629

Katharine A. Munning, Ph.D.
Assistant Professor
Duke — Watts Family Medicine
    Program
407 Crutchfield Street
Durham, NC 27704
(919) 471-2571

Glenn F. Nyre, Ph.D.
Vice President and Executive
    Director
Evaluation and Training
    Institute
12401 Wilshire Boulevard
Suite 304
Los Angeles, CA 90025
(213) 820-8521

Sheryl Riechmann, Ph.D.
University of
    Massachusetts — Amherst
HS/ABS

Prepared by Sylvia L. Sharma, Ph.D. and Donald K. Polloch, American Association of Colleges of Osteopathic Medicine, Washington, D.C. Faculty Assessment Project funded by DHEW Contract No. 231-77-0066.

477 Hills South
Amherst, MA 01003
(413) 545-0868

Clare Rose, Ph.D., President
Evaluation and Training
  Institute
12401 Wilshire Boulevard
Suite 304
Los Angeles, CA 90025
(213) 820-8521

Stephen L. Yelon, Ph.D.
Professor and Assistant
  Director
Michigan State University
17 Morrill Hall
East Lansing, MI 48824
(517) 353-8942

Robert E. Young, Ph.D.
Assistant Director for
  Instructional Development
Virginia Commonwealth
  University
310 West Franklin Street
Richmond, VA 23284
(804) 257-1121

B. Medical Education

Stephen Abrahamson, M.D.
Director
Division of Research in
  Medical Education
University of Southern
  California
School of Medicine
2025 Zonal Avenue
Los Angeles, CA 90033
(213) 225-2038

Philip Bashook, Ed.D.

Associate Director
Educational Development Unit
Michael Reese School of Health
  Science
530 East 31st
Chicago, IL 60616
(312) 791-5530

Carole Bland, Ph.D.
Associate Professor
Department of Family Practice
  and Community Health
University of Minnesota
Medical School
Box 381 Mayo
516 Delaware Street, SE
Minneapolis, MN 55455
(612) 376-3689
(612) 376-3317

Wayne K. Davis, Ph.D.,
  Director
Office of Educational
  Resources and Research
University of Michigan
G 1111 Towsley Center
Ann Arbor, MI 48109
(313) 763-1153

Charles W. Dohner, Ph.D.
Associate Professor
Office of Research in Medical
  Education
University of Washington
School of Medicine
E-312 Health Sciences
  Building, SC-45
Seattle, WA 98195
(206) 543-2259

Lawrence A. Fisher, Ph.D.
Director, DEPA

Faculty of Medicine
University of Calgary
Calgary, Alberta
Canada T2N 1N4
(403) 284-6845

Merrel D. Flair, Ph.D.,
  Director,
Office of Medical Studies
Professor Department of
  Psychiatry,
School of Medicine
Clinical Professor, School of
  Education
University of North Carolina
School of Medicine
Chapel Hill, NC 27514
(919) 966-4461

Richard E. Gallagher, Ph.D.
Director, Division of
  Educational Services and
  Research
Wayne State University
540 East Canfield Avenue
Detroit, MI 48201
(313) 577-1378

Robert H. Geertsma, Ph.D.
Professor and Chairman,
  Division of Medical
  Education and
  Communication
Professor, Psychiatry
  Department and Graduate
  School of Education and
  Human Development
University of Rochester
School of Medicine and
  Dentistry
250 Crittenden Boulevard

Rochester, NY 14642
(716) 275-2928

Rhonda M. Goldberg, M.A.
Associate Director of Education
George Washington University
  School of Medicine and
  Health Sciences
713 Ross Hall
2300 I Street, NW
Washington, DC 20037
(202) 676-2977

Ilene B. Harris, M.A.
Research Associate
University of Minnesota
  Medical School Curriculum
  Affairs
Box 33 Mayo
421 Delaware St. SE
Minneapolis, MN 55455
(612) 376-7241

Robert S. Jackson, Ph.D.
President and Founder
Robert Jackson and Associates
845 Chicago Avenue
Evanston, IL 60202
(312) 475-1166

Harry J. Knopke, Ph.D.
Director, Office of Educational
  Development
College of Community Health
  Sciences
P.O. Box 6291
University, AL 35486
(205) 348-7942

Larry Lambert, Ed.D.
Director of Educational
  Development

University of Tennessee Center
for Health Sciences
Memphis, TN 38163
(901) 528-6392

Harold G. Levine, M.P.A.
Director, Office of Research in
Medical Education
The University of Texas
Medical Branch
114 Keiller Building
Galveston, TX 77550
(713) 765-2791

Maurice Levy, Ed.D.
Professor of Educational
Research and Development
Coordinator for Educational
Planning
Medical College of Georgia
Augusta, GA 30902
(404) 828-2703

Marilyn Margon, M.A.
Coordinator of Educational
Development
Montefiore Hospital
3329 Rochambeau Avenue
Bronx, NY 10467
(212) 920-5524, 5521

Judith K. Peretz, M.S.,
Director,
Curriculum and Faculty
Development
New York College of
Osteopathic Medicine
P.O. Box 170
Wheatley Road
Old Westbury, NY 11568
(516) 686-7724

Ruth Scheuer, M.P.H.
Director of Program Evaluation
Sophie Davis School for
Biomedical Education
The City College of New York
138th and Convent Avenue,
Room 910J
New York, NY 10031
(212) 690-8255-6-7

Winfield H. Scott, Ph.D.
Associate Dean for Education
Director, Office of Education
George Washington University
School of Medicine and Health
Sciences
713 Ross Hall
2300 I Street, NW
Washington, DC 20037
(202) 676-2977

David L. Silber, M.D.
Assistant Dean
Curriculum Affairs and
Educational Resources
Southern Illinois University
School of Medicine
Springfield, IL 62702
(217) 782-7878

Gregory L. Trzebiatowski,
Ph.D.
Associate Dean for Medical
and Graduate Education
Ohio State University College
of Medicine
254 Medical Administration
Center
370 West 9th Avenue
Columbus, OH 43210
(614) 422-6437

EVALUATION

A. Higher Education

Lawrence Aleamoni, Ph.D.
Director
Instructional Research and
  Development
University of Arizona
Tucson, AZ 85721
(602) 626-4488

William Bergquist, Ph.D.
Consultant
1217 Campus Drive
Berkeley, CA 94708
(415) 845-2299

Susan A. Brock, Ph.D.
Coordinator of Faculty
  Development
St. Mary's Junior College
2500 South 6th Street
Minneapolis, MN 55454
(612) 332-5521

John Centra, Ph.D.
Senior Research Psychologist
Educational Testing Service
Rosedale Road
Princeton, NJ 08540
(609) 921-9000

Lawrence Demarest, Ph.D.
Director of Educational
  Development and Evaluation
St. Mary's Junior College
2500 South 6th Street
Minneapolis, MN 55454
(612) 332-5521

Paul L. Dressel, Ph.D.
Professor of University
  Research

Michigan State University
Room 331
Hannah Administration
  Building
East Lansing, MI 48824
(517) 355-6629

Tony Grasha, Ph.D.
Associate Professor of
  Psychology
University of Cincinnati
Department of Psychology
McMickon Hall
Cincinnati, OH 45208
(513) 475-2228
(513) 475-3631

Sam H. Lane, Ph.D.
Senior Associate
Projects for Educational
  Development
1836 Euclid Avenue, No. 203
Cleveland, OH 44115

Irvin Lehmann, Ph.D.,
  Consultant
Learning and Evaluation
  Service
Michigan State University
206 South Kedzie
East Lansing, MI 48824
(517) 355-3408

Ronald Lippitt, Ph.D.
President, Human Resources
  Development Associates
Professor Emeritus, Sociology
  and Psychology, University of
  Michigan
Human Resources Development
  Association

1916 Cambridge Road
Ann Arbor, MI 48104
(313) 663-4740
(313) 994-4616

Christine McGuire, M.A.
Associate Director
Center for Educational
  Development
University of Illinois
808 South Wood Street
Chicago, IL 60612
(312) 996-3000

Charles A. McKee, Ed.D.
Cranbrook Learning Associates
1094 Haslett Road
Haslett, MI 48840

James Nord, Ph.D., Consultant
Learning and Evaluation
  Service
Michigan State University
17 Morrill Hall
East Lansing, MI 48824
(517) 353-4644

Joan North, Ph.D., Director
Professional Development
Small Colleges Consortium
2000 P Street, NW, No. 400
Washington, DC 20036
(202) 223-6080

Glenn F. Nyre, Ph.D.
Vice President and Executive
  Director
Evaluation and Training
  Institute
12401 Wilshire Boulevard
Suite 304
Los Angeles, CA 90025

(213) 820-8521

LeRoy Olson, Ph.D.,
  Consultant
Learning and Evaluation
  Service
Michigan State University
202 South Kedzie
East Lansing, MI 48824
(517) 355-3408

W. James Potter, Ph.D.
Assistant Director for
  Evaluation and Research
Virginia Commonwealth
  University
310 North Shafer Street
Richmond, VA 23284
(804) 257-1121

Gary H. Quehl, President
Council for the Advancement
  of Small Colleges
One Dupont Circle, NW
Washington, DC 20036
(202) 659-3795

Sheryl Riechmann, Ph.D.
University of
  Massachusetts — Amherst
HS/ABS
477 Hills South
Amherst, MA 01003
(413) 545-0868

Clare Rose, Ph.D., President
Evaluation and Training
  Institute
12401 Wilshire Boulevard
Suite 304
Los Angeles, CA 90025
(213) 820-8521

Stephen Scholl, Ph.D., Dean
Educational Services
Ohio Wesleyan University
Academic Affairs Office U-107
Delaware, OH 43015
(614) 369-4431, ext. 710

B. Medical Education

Stephen Abrahamson, M.D.,
    Director
Division of Research in Medical
    Education
University of Southern
    California
School of Medicine
2025 Zonal Avenue
Los Angeles, CA 90033
(213) 226-2038

Philip Bashook, Ed.D.
Associate Director
Educational Development Unit
Michael Reese School of Health
    Sciences
530 East 31st
Chicago, IL 60616
(312) 791-5530

Carole Bland, Ph.D.
Associate Professor
Department of Family Practice
    and Community Health
University of Minnesota
Medical School
Box 381 Mayo
516 Delaware Street, SE
Minneapolis, MN 55455
(612) 376-3689
(612) 376-3317

James Bobula, Ph.D.

Director of Education and
    Evaluation
Department of Family Practice
Duke — Watts Family Medicine
    Program
407 Crutchfield Street
Durham, NC 27704
(919) 471-2571

Sam Brown, Ed.D., Director
Office of Educational
    Development
University of Alabama
School of Medicine
Box 332, NBSB, University
    Station
Birmingham, AL 35294
(205) 943-3053

Wayne K. Davis, Ph.D.,
    Director
Office of Educational
    Resources and Research
University of Michigan
G 1111 Towsley Center
Ann Arbor, MI 48109
(313) 763-1153

James Erdmann, Ph.D.,
    Director
Division of Educational
    Measurement and Research
Association of American
    Medical Colleges
One Dupont Circle
Washington, DC 20036
(202) 466-5166

Merrel D. Flair, Ph.D.,
    Director
Office of Medical Studies
Professor Department of

Psychiatry,
School of Medicine
Clinical Professor, School of
    Education
University of North Carolina
School of Medicine
Chapel Hill, NC 27514
(919) 966-4461

Richard E. Gallagher, Ph.D.
Director, Division of
    Educational Services and
    Research
Wayne State University
540 East Canfield Avenue
Detroit, MI 48201
(313) 577-1378

Robert H. Geertsma, Ph.D.
Professor and Chairman,
    Division of Medical
    Education and
    Communication
Professor, Psychiatry
    Department and Graduate
    School of Education and
    Human Development
University of Rochester
School of Medicine and
    Dentistry
250 Crittenden Boulevard
Rochester, NY 14642
(716) 275-2928

Rhonda M. Goldberg, M.A.
Associate Director of Education
George Washington University
School of Medicine and Health
    Sciences
713 Ross Hall
2300 I Street, NW

Washington, DC 20037
(202) 676-2977

Michael J. Gordon, Ph.D.
Research Assistant Professor
Office of Research in Medical
    Education
University of Washington
School of Medicine
Seattle, WA 98195
(206) 543-9425

Ilene B. Harris, M.A.
Research Associate
University of Minnesota
    Medical School Curriculum
    Affairs
Box 33 Mayo
421 Delaware St. SE
Minneapolis, MN 55455
(612) 376-7241

David M. Irby, Ph.D.,
    Director, Training Programs
Office of Research in Medical
    Education
University of Washington
School of Medicine
Seattle, WA 98195
(206) 543-3891

Judith Kaplan, M.A.
Research Specialist
New Jersey Medical School
100 Bergen Street
Newark, NJ 07103
(201) 456-4823

Harry J. Knopke, Ph.D.
Director, Office of Educational
    Development
College of Community Health

Sciences
P.O. Box 6291
University, AL 35486
(205) 348-7942

Sandra L. Lass, Ph.D.
Research Associate
Department of Medical
  Education
USC School of Medicine
2025 Zonal Avenue
Los Angeles, CA 90033
(213) 226-2038
(714) 597-2900

Maurice Levy, Ed.D.
Professor of Educational
  Research and Development
Coordinator for Educational
  Planning
Medical College of Georgia
Augusta, GA 30902
(404) 828-2703

William L. Logan, Ph.D.,
  Director
Center for Educational
  Development and Evaluation
East Carolina University
Division of Health Affairs
School of Medicine
Greenville, NC 27834
(919) 757-6157

Marilyn Margon, M.A.
Coordinator of Educational
  Development
Montefiore Hospital
3329 Rochambeau Avenue
Bronx, NY 10467
(212) 920-5524, 5521

Jack Mason, Ph.D., Assistant
  Dean for Continuing Medical
  Education
University of Maryland School
  of Medicine
Room 300, MSTF
10 South Pine Street
Baltimore, MD 21201
(301) 528-3956

Merlin Mitchell, Ed.D.
Head — Instructional
  Development Unit
Mayo Medical School
212 Student Center
Rochester, MN 55901
(507) 284-3978

Gordon Page, Ed.D., Director
Division of Educational
  Support and Development
Office of the Coordinator of
  Health Sciences
University of British Columbia
Vancouver, British Columbia
Canada V6T 1W5
(604) 228-6641

Judith K. Peretz, M.S.
Director of Curriculum and
  Faculty Development
New York College of
  Osteopathic Medicine
P.O. Box 170
Wheatley Road
Old Westbury, NY 11568
(516) 686-7724

William G. Pfeifle, Ed.D.
Project Director of Teaching
  Improvement
Project System and Health

Care Educators
University of Kentucky
Medical Annex 3
Lexington, KY 40506
(606) 233-5616

Ruth Scheuer, M.P.H.,
  Director of Program
  Evaluation
Sophie Davis School for
  Biomedical Education
The City College of New York
138th and Convent Avenue,
  Room 910J
New York, NY 10031
(212) 690-8255-6-7

Frank Schimpfhauser, Ph.D.
Assistant Dean for Medical
  Education
Director, Research and
  Evaluation in Medical
  Education
S.U.N.Y. at Buffalo
140 Farber Hall
Buffalo, NY 14214
(716) 831-2811

Mitchell Schorow, Ph.D.
Coordinator for Educational
  Development
Columbia University College of
  Physicians and Surgeons
630 West 168th Street
New York, NY 10032
(212) 694-3827

Hugh Scott, M.D., Professor
  and Chairman, Department
  of Medicine
Centre Hospitalier Universitaire
Sherbrooke, Quebec J1H 5N4

(819) 563-5555 #252

Winfield H. Scott, Ph.D.
Associate Dean for Education
Director, Office of Education
George Washington University
School of Medicine and Health
  Sciences
713 Ross Hall
2300 I Street, NW
Washington, DC 20037
(202) 676-2977

T. Joseph Sheehan, Ph.D.
Professor and Head,
  Department of Research in
  Health Education
University of Connecticut
  Health Center
Schools of Medicine and Dental
  Medicine
Farmington, CT 06032
(203) 674-2118

Howard L. Stone, Ph.D.,
  Director
Office of Educational
  Resources
University of
  Wisconsin — Madison
427 Lorch Court
Madison, WI 53706
(608) 263-4714

Bruce Strem, Ph.D., Director
Research in Dental Education
Georgetown University
School of Dentistry
Washington, DC 20007
(202) 625-7283

Melvin S. Swanson, Ph.D.

Associate Director for
Evaluation
Center for Educational
Development and Evaluation
East Carolina University
School of Medicine
Greenville, NC 27834
(919) 757-6157

Gregory L. Trzebiatowski,
Ph.D.
Associate Dean for Medical
and Graduate Education
Ohio State University College
of Medicine
254 Medical Administration
Center
370 West 9th Avenue
Columbus, OH 43210
(614) 422-6437

Leslie Walker-Bartnick, M.A.
Research Analyst
University of Maryland School
of Medicine
10 South Pine Street,

Room 334
Baltimore, MD 21201
(301) 528-6613

Jon F. Wergin, Ph.D.,
Associate Professor
Educational Planning and
Development Program
Virginia Commonwealth
University
Medical College of Virginia
Campus
MCV Station Box 124
Richmond, VA 23298
(804) 786-9778

Theodore W. Whitley, Ph.D.
Assistant Director
Center for Educational
Development and Evaluation
East Carolina University
School of Medicine
Greenville, NC 27834
(919) 757-6157
(919) 756-8742

FACULTY DEVELOPMENT

A. Higher Education

Lawrence Aleamoni, Ph.D.
Director
Instructional Research and
Development
University of Arizona
Tucson, AZ 84721
(602) 626-4488

William Bergquist, Ph.D.
Consultant
1217 Campus Drive
Berkeley, CA 94708

(415) 845-2299

Bert R. Biles, Ph.D.
Special Assistant for Sponsored
Programs
The Graduate School
Fairchild Hall
Kansas State University
Manhattan, KS 66506
(913) 532-6194
(913) 537-9400

Lance Buhl, Ph.D.
President

Projects for Educational
   Development
1836 Euclid Avenue, No. 203
Cleveland, OH 44115
(216) 241-7586

Mary Lynn Crow, Ph.D.
Director of Faculty
   Development
University of Texas at Arlington
Suite 2 Library Basement
Arlington, TX 76019
(817) 273-3339

Robert H. Davis, Ph.D.,
   Director
Educational Development
   Program
Michigan State University
17 Morrill Hall
East Lansing, MI 48824
(517) 332-6855

John Fry, Ph.D.
Consultant
Learning and Evaluation
   Service
Michigan State University
17 Morrill Hall
East Lansing, MI 48824
(517) 353-4643

Jerry Gaff, Ph.D.
Project Director
Project on Institutional Renewal
   Through the Improvement of
   Teaching
1818 R Street, NW
Washington, DC 20009
(202) 462-4846

Frederick H. Gaige, Ph.D.,

Dean
Fairleigh Dickinson
   University
College of Arts and Sciences
Madison, NJ 07940
(201) 377-4700, ext. 339

Tony Grasha, Ph.D.
Associate Professor of
   Psychology
University of Cincinnati
Department of Psychology
McMickon Hall
Cincinnati, OH 45208
(513) 475-2288
(513) 475-3631

Sam H. Lane, Ph.D.
Senior Associate
Projects for Educational
   Development
1836 Euclid Avenue, No. 203
Cleveland, OH 44115

B. Claude Mathis, Ph.D.
Director
Center for the Teaching
   Professions
Northwestern University
2003 Sheridan Road
Evanston, IL 60201
(312) 492-3620

Charles A. McKee, Ed.D.
Cranbrook Learning Associates
1094 Haslett Road
Haslett, MI 48840

Merlin Mitchell, Ed.D.
Head — Instructional
   Development Unit
Mayo Medical School

212 Student Center
Rochester, MN 55901
(507) 284-3978

Al P. Mizell, Ed.D., Director
Curriculum Design
Nova University
3301 College Avenue
Fort Lauderdale, FL 33314
(305) 587-6660, ext. 340
(305) 962-7872

Glenn F. Nyre, Ph.D.
Vice President and Executive
  Director
Evaluation and Training
  Institute
12401 Wilshire Boulevard,
  Suite 304
Los Angeles, CA 90025
(213) 820-8521

Steven R. Phillips, Ph.D.
Director
Associated Schools of the Pacific
  Northwest
University of Puget Sound
1500 North Warner
Tacoma, WA 98407

W. James Potter, Ph.D.
Assistant Director for
Evaluation and Research
Virginia Commonwealth
University
310 North Shafer Street
Richmond, VA 23284
(804) 257-1121

Gary H. Quehl, Ph.D.,
  President
Council for the Advancement of
  Small Colleges

One Dupont Circle, NW
Washington, DC 20036
(212) 659-3795

Sheryl Riechmann, Ph.D.
University of Massachusetts-
  Amherst
HS/ABS
477 Hills South
Amherst, MA 01003
(413) 545-0868

Clare Rose, Ph.D., President
Evaluation and Training
  Institute
12401 Wilshire Boulevard,
  Suite 304
Los Angeles, CA 90025
(213) 820-8521

Mitchell Schorow, Ph.D.
Coordinator for Educational
  Development
Columbia University College
  of Physicians and Surgeons
630 West 168th Street
New York, NY 10032
(212) 694-3827

Walter Sikes, Ph.D.
Consultant
Center for Creative Change in
  Higher Education
111 West North College
Yellow Springs, OH 45387
(513) 767-7029

Albert B. Smith, III, Ph.D.
Associate Professor, Higher
  Education, Curriculum and
  Instruction
College of Education

University of Florida
Gainesville, FL 32601

Marilla D. Svinicki, Ph.D.
Assistant Director
Center for Teaching
 Effectiveness
University of Texas at Austin
Main 2202
Austin, TX 78712
(512) 471-1488

Luann Wilkerson, Ed.D.
Director, Center for
 Enhancement of Teaching
 Effectiveness
Murray State University
Lowry Center
Murray, KY 42071
(502) 762-2535

Robert E. Young, Ph.D.
Assistant Director for
 Instructional Development
Virginia Commonwealth
 University
310 West Franklin Street
Richmond, VA 23284
(804) 257-1121

Carol Zion, Ph.D., Director,
Management and Organization
 Development
Miami-Dade Community
 College
11380 Northwest 27th Avenue
Miami, FL 33167
(305) 685-4514

B. Medical Education

Stephen Abrahamson, M.D.,
 Director

Division of Research in Medical
 Education
University of Southern
 California
School of Medicine
2025 Zonal Avenue
Los Angeles, CA 90033
(213) 226-2038

Neal Balanoff, Ph.D., Director
Learning Resources Center
University of Florida
Box J-16 JHM Health Center
Gainesville, FL 32610
(904) 392-4151

Philip Bashook, Ed.D.
Associate Director
Educational Development Unit
Michael Reese School of Health
 Science
530 East 31st
Chicago, IL 60616
(312) 791-5530

Carole Bland, Ph.D.
Associate Professor
Department of Family Practice
 and Community Health
University of Minnesota
Medical School
Box 381 Mayo
516 Delaware Street, SE
Minneapolis, MN 55455
(612) 376-3689
(612) 376-3317

James Bobula, Ph.D., Director,
 Education and Evaluation
Department of Family Practice
Duke—Watts Family Medicine
 Program

Durham, NC 27706
(919) 471-2571

T. Earle Bowen, Jr., Ph.D.
Assistant Vice Chancellor for
Academic Affairs
University of Tennessee Center
Health Sciences
800 Madison Avenue
Memphis, TN 38163
(901) 528-5578

Sam Brown, Ed.D., Director
Office of Educational
Development
University of Alabama
School of Medicine
Box 332, NBSB, University
Station
Birmingham, AL 35294
(205) 943-3053

D. Joseph Clark, Ph.D.,
Director
Biological Sciences Learning
Resource Center
University of Washington
Johnson Annex A AK-15
Seattle, WA 98195
(206) 543-6588

Rhonda Goldberg, M.A.
Associate Director for Education
George Washington University
School of Medicine and
Health Sciences
713 Ross Hall
2300 I Street, NW
Washington, DC 20037
(202) 676-2977

Michael J. Gordon, Ph.D.
Research Assistant Professor

Office of Research in Medical
Education
University of Washington
School of Medicine
Seattle, WA 98195
(206) 543-9425

Ilene B. Harris, M.A.
Research Associate
University of Minnesota Medical
School Curriculum Affairs
Box 33 Mayo
421 Delaware St. SE
Minneapolis, MN 55455
(612) 376-7241

Sandra Inglis, Ed.D., Director
Educational Development and
Resources
College of Osteopathic Medicine
Ohio University
Athens, OH 45701
(614) 594-6401 ext. 275

David M. Irby, Ph.D., Director,
Training Programs
Office of Research in Medical
Education
University of Washington
School of Medicine
Seattle, WA 98195
(206) 543-3891

Hilliard Jason, M.D., Director
National Center for Faculty
Development
University of Miami School of
Medicine
P.O. Box 016960
Miami, FL 33101
(305) 661-7340

Maurice Levy, Ed.D.

Professor of Educational
   Research and Development
Coordinator for Educational
   Planning
Medical College of Georgia
Augusta, GA 30902
(404) 828-2703

Marilyn Margon, M.A.
Coordinator   of   Educational
   Development
Montefiore Hospital
3329 Rochambeau Avenue
Bronx, NY 10467
(212) 920-5524, 5521

Jack Mason, Ph.D.
Assistant Dean for Continuing
   Medical Education
University of Maryland School
   of Medicine
Room 300, MSTF
10 South Pine Street
Baltimore, MD 21201
(301) 528-3956

Paul R. Mehne, Ph.D.
Associate Director for
   Development
Center for Educational
   Development and Evaluation
East Carolina University
School of Medicine
Greenville, NC 27834
(919) 757-6157

C. Benjamin Meleca, Ph.D.,
   Director and Associate
   Professor, Division of
   Research and Evaluation in
   Medical Education
Ohio State University

School of Medicine
3190 Graves Hall
Columbus, OH 43210
(614) 422-9063

Katherine A. Munning, Ph.D.
Assistant Professor
Duke — Watts Family Medicine
   Program
407 Crutchfield Street
Durham, NC 27704
(919) 471-2571

Paul J. Munson, Ed.D.,
   Professor
Educational   Planning   and
   Development Program
Medical   College   of   Virginia
   Campus
Virginia   Commonwealth
   University
MCV Station Box 124
Richmond, VA 23298
(804) 786-9779

William G. Pfeifle, Ed.D.
Project   Director   of   Teaching
   Improvement
Project System and Health Care
   Educators
University of Kentucky
Medical Annex 3
Lexington, KY 40506
(606) 233-5616

Gregory   L.   Trzebiatowski,
   Ph.D.
Associate Dean for Medical and
   Graduate Education
Ohio State University College of
   Medicine
254   Medical   Administration

Center
370 West 9th Avenue
Columbus, OH 43210
(614) 422-6437

Eugenia Vanek, Ed.D.
Division of Research in Medical
  Education
Case Western Reserve University
School of Medicine
2119 Abington Road
Cleveland, OH 44106

Jon F. Wergin, Ph.D.
Associate Professor
Educational Planning and
  Development Program
Medical College of Virginia
  Campus
Virginia Commonwealth
  University
MCV Station Box 124
Richmond, VA 23298
(804) 786-9778

Jane Westberg, M.A.
Associate Director
National Center for Faculty

Development
University of Miami School of
  Medicine
P.O. Box 016960
Miami, FL 33101
(305) 661-7340

Loren Williams, Ph.D.
Professor and Director
Educational Planning and
  Development Program
Medical College of Virginia
  Campus
Virginia Commonwealth
  University
MCV Station Box 124
Richmond, VA 23298
(804) 786-9781

Muriel Wolkow, Ed.D.
Research Associate
Department of Medical
  Education
USC School of Medicine
2025 Zonal Avenue
Los Angeles, CA 90033

INSTRUCTIONAL DESIGN

A. Higher Education

Lawrence Aleamoni, Ph.D.
Instructional Research and
  Development
University of Arizona
Tucson, AZ 85721
(602) 626-4488

Lawrence T. Alexander, Ph.D.
Professor and Director
Learning and Evaluation
  Service

Michigan State University
17 Morrill Hall
East Lansing, MI 48824
(517) 353-8940

William Bergquist, Ph.D.
1217 Campus Drive
Berkeley, CA 94708
(415) 845-2299

Bert R. Biles, Ph.D.
Special Assistant for Sponsored
  Programs

The Graduate School
Fairchild Hall
Kansas State University
Manhattan, KS 66506
(913) 532-6194
(913) 537-9400

Mary Lynn Crow, Ph.D.
Director of Faculty
  Development
University of Texas at
  Arlington
Suite 2 Library Basement
Arlington, TX 76019
(817) 273-3339

Robert M. Diamond, Ph.D.
Assistant Vice Chancellor
Center for Instructional
  Development
Syracuse University
115 College Place
Syracuse, NY 13210
(315) 423-4571

Richard Fenker, Jr., Ph.D.
Professor of Psychology
Texas Christian University
Fort Worth, TX 76129
(817) 921-7000 ext. 6416

John Fry, Ph.D.
Consultant
Learning and Evaluation
  Service
Michigan State University
17 Morrill Hall
East Lansing, MI 48824
(517) 353-4643

Tony Grasha, Ph.D.
Associate Professor of

Psychology
University of Cincinnati
Department of Psychology
McMickon Hall
Cincinnati, OH 45208
(513) 475-2228
(513) 475-3531

Sam H. Lane, Ph.D.
Senior Associate
Projects for Educational
  Development
1836 Euclid Avenue, No. 203
Cleveland, OH 44115

B. Claude Mathis, Ph.D.,
  Director
Center for the Teaching
  Professions
Northwestern University
2003 Sheridan Road
Evanston, IL 60201
(312) 492-3620

Al P. Mizell, Ed.D., Director
Curriculum Design
Nova University
3301 College Avenue
Fort Lauderdale, FL 33314
(305) 587-6660, ext. 340
(305) 962-7872

James Nord, Ph.D., Consultant
Learning and Evaluation
  Service
Michigan State University
17 Morrill Hall
East Lansing, MI 48824
(517) 353-4644

Glenn F. Nyre, Ph.D.
Vice President and Executive

Director
Evaluation and Training
  Institute
12401 Wilshire Boulevard
Suite 304
Los Angeles, CA 90025
(213) 820-8521

David L. Outcalt, Ph.D., Dean
Instructional Development
University of California, Santa
  Barbara
Santa Barbara, CA 93106
(805) 961-3945

W. James Potter, Ph.D.
Assistant Director for
  Evaluation and Research
Virginia Commonwealth
  University
310 North Shafer Street
Richmond, VA 23284
(804) 257-1121

Sheryl Riechmann, Ph.D.
University of
  Massachusetts — Amherst
HS/ABS
477 Hills South
Amherst, MA 01003
(413) 545-0868

Clare Rose, Ph.D., President
Evaluation and Training
  Institute
12401 Wilshire Boulevard
Suite 304
Los Angeles, CA 90025
(213) 820-8521

Mitchell Schorow, Ph.D.
Coordinator for Educational

Development
Columbia University College of
  Physicians and Surgeons
630 West 168th Street
New York, NY 10032
(212) 694-3827

Marilla D. Svinicki, Ph.D.
Assistant Director
Center for Teaching
  Effectiveness
University of Texas at Austin
Main 2202
Austin, TX 78712
(512) 471-1488

Luann Wilkerson, Ed.D.
Director, Center for
  Enhancement of Teaching
  Effectiveness
Murray State University
Lowry Center
Murray, KY 42071
(502) 762-2535

Stephen L. Yelon, Ph.D.
Professor and Assistant
  Director
Michigan State University
17 Morrill Hall
East Lansing, MI 48824
(517) 353-8942

Robert E. Young, Ph.D.
Assistant Director for
  Instructional Development
Virginia Commonwealth
  University
310 West Franklin Street
Richmond, VA 23284
(804) 257-1121

Eric Zemper, M.S.

Consultant
Learning and Evaluation
  Service
Michigan State University
202 South Kedzie
East Lansing, MI 48824
(517) 355-3408

B. Medical Education

D. Joseph Clark, Ph.D.,
  Director
Biological Sciences Learning
  Resource Center
University of Washington
Johnson Annex A AK-15
Seattle, WA 98195
(206) 543-6588

Robert H. Geertsma, Ph.D.
Professor and Chairman
  Division of Medical
  Education and
  Communication
Professor, Psychiatry
  Department and Graduate
  School of Education and
  Human Development
University of Rochester
School of Medicine and
  Dentistry
250 Crittenden Boulevard
Rochester, NY 14642
(716) 275-2928

Raymond Genick, Ph.D.
Assistant Dean of Development
College Lifelong Learning
Wayne State University
Detroit, MI 48202
(313) 557-4677

Ed Glassman, Ph.D.

Professor of Biochemistry
Medical School
Chapel Hill, NC 27514
(919) 966-3163

Michael J. Gordon, Ph.D.
Research Assistant Professor
Office of Research in Medical
  Education
University of Washington
School of Medicine
Seattle, WA 98195
(206) 543-9425

Robert S. Jackson, Ph.D.
President and Founder
Robert Jackson and Associates
845 Chicago Avenue
Evanston, IL 60202
(312) 475-1166

Harry J. Knopke, Ph.D.
Director, Office of Educational
  Development
College of Community Health
  Sciences
P.O. Box 6291
University, AL 35486
(205) 348-7942

Larry Lambert, Ed.D.
Director of Educational
  • Development
University of Tennessee Center
  for Health Sciences
Memphis, TN 38163
(901) 528-6392

William L. Logan, Ph.D.,
  Director
Center for Educational
  Development and Evaluation
East Carolina University

Division of Health Affairs
School of Medicine
Greenville, NC 27834
(919) 757-6157

Jack Mason, Ph.D., Assistant
 Dean for Continuing Medical
 Education

University of Maryland School
 of Medicine
Room 300, MSTF
10 South Pine Street
Baltimore, MD 21201
(301) 528-3956

Paul R. Mehne, Ph.D.
Associate Director for
 Development
Center for Educational
 Development and Evaluation
School of Medicine
East Carolina University
Greenville, NC 27834
(919) 757-6157

Paul J. Munson, Ed.D.,
 Professor
Educational Planning and
 Development Program
Medical College of Virginia
 Campus
Virginia Commonwealth
 University
MCV Station Box 124
Richmond, VA 23298
(804) 786-9779

Robert Reichart, Ed.D.
Director, Office of Medical
 Education
University of Oregon Medical
 School
3181 South West Sam Jackson
 Park Road
Portland, OR 97201
(503) 225-8430

David L. Silber, M.D.
Assistant Dean
Curriculum Affairs and
 Educational Resources
Southern Illinois University
School of Medicine
Springfield, IL 62702
(217) 782-7878

Gregory L. Trzebiatowski,
 Ph.D.
Associate Dean for Medical
 and Graduate Education
Ohio State University College
 of Medicine
254 Medical Administration
 Center
370 West 9th Avenue
Columbus, OH 43210
(614) 422-6437

Eugenia Vanek, Ed.D.
Division of Research in Medical
 Education
Case Western Reserve
 University
School of Medicine
2119 Abington Road
Cleveland, OH 44106

INSTRUCTIONAL TECHNOLOGY

A. Higher Education

Neal Balanoff, Ph.D., Director

Learning Resources Center
University of Florida

Box J-16
JHM Health Center
Gainesville, FL 32610
(904) 392-4151

William Bergquist, Ph.D.
Consultant
1217 Campus Drive
Berkeley, CA 94708
(415) 845-2299

Tom Held, Ed.D.
Director of Media
University of Maryland School
   of Medicine
Baltimore, MD 21201
(301) 528-3956

Merlin Mitchell, Ed.D.
Head — Instructional
   Development Unit
Mayo Medical School
212 Student Center
Rochester, MN 55901
(507) 284-3978

Al P. Mizell, Ed.D., Director
Curriculum Design
Nova University
3301 College Avenue
Fort Lauderdale, FL 33314
(305) 587-6660, ext. 340
(305) 962-7872

B. Medical Education

D. Joseph Clark, Ph.D.,
   Director
Biological Sciences Learning
   Resource Center
University of Washington
Johnson Annex A AK-15

Seattle, WA 98195
(206) 543-6588

Robert S. Jackson, Ph.D.
President and Founder
Robert Jackson and Associates
845 Chicago Avenue
Evanston, IL 60202
(312) 475-1166

Ruth Scheuer, M.P.H.
Director of Program Evaluation
Sophie Davis School for
   Biomedical Education
The City College of New York
138th and Convent Avenue,
   Room 910J
New York, NY 10031
(212) 690-8255-6-7

Frank Schimpfhauser, Ph.D.
Assistant Dean for Medical
   Education
Director, Research and
   Evaluation in Medical
   Education
S.U.N.Y. at Buffalo
140 Farber Hall
Buffalo, NY 14214
(716) 831-2811

Robert F. Schuck, Ed.D.
Assistant Dean, School of
   Medicine and Director,
   D.R.M.E.
University of Pittsburgh School
   of Medicine
M-249 Scaife Hall
Pittsburgh, PA 15261
(412) 624-2656

MEDICAL EDUCATION

A. Higher Education

Jane Westberg, M.A.
Associate Director
National Center For Faculty
  Development
University of Miami School of
  Medicine
P.O. Box 016960
Miami, FL 33101
(305) 661-7340

B. Medical Education

Sarah M. Dinham, Ph.D.
Director, Office of Medical
  Education
University of Arizona College
  of Medicine
Tucson, AZ 85724
(602) 882-6707

Charles W. Dohner, Ph.D.
Associate Professor
Office of Research in Medical
  Education
University of Washington
School of Medicine
E-312 Health Sciences
  Building, SC-45
Seattle, WA 98195
(206) 543-2259

Merrel D. Flair, Ph.D.
Director
Office of Medical Studies
Professor Department of
  Psychiatry
School of Medicine
Clinical Professor, School of
  Education
University of North Carolina

School of Medicine
Chapel Hill, NC 27514
(919) 966-4461

Richard E. Gallagher, Ph.D.
Director, Division of
  Educational Services and
  Research
Wayne State University
540 East Canfield Avenue
Detroit, MI 48201
(313) 577-1378

Murray Kappelman, M.D.
Associate Dean, Medical
  Education and Special
  Programs
Professor, Pediatrics
Office of Medical Education
University of Maryland School
  of Medicine
Baltimore, MD 21201
(301) 528-7476

Harold G. Levine, M.P.A.
Director, Office of Research in
  Medical Education
The University of Texas
  Medical Branch
114 Keiller Building
Galveston, TX 77550
(713) 765-2791

C. Benjamin Meleca, Ph.D.
Director and Associate
  Professor, Division of
  Research and Evaluation in
  Medical Education
Ohio State University
School of Medicine
3190 Graves Hall

Columbus, OH 43210
(614) 422-9063

Donald Pochyly, M.D.
Provost and Acting President

University Health Sciences,
    Chicago Medical School
2020 West Ogden
Chicago, IL 60612
(312) 226-4100

ORGANIZATIONAL DEVELOPMENT

A. Higher Education

William Bergquist, Ph.D.
Consultant
1217 Campus Drive
Berkeley, CA 94708
(415) 845-2299

Susan A. Brock, Ph.D.
Coordinator of Faculty
    Development
St. Mary's Junior College
2500 South 6th Street
Minneapolis, MN 55454
(612) 332-5521

Lance Buhl, Ph.D.
President
Projects for Educational
    Development
1836 Euclid Avenue, No. 203
Cleveland, OH 44115
(216) 241-7586

Kendall Cowing, Ph.D.
Executive Director
Human Resource Development
    Associates
1820 Green Road
Ann Arbor, MI 48105
(313) 994-4616

Robert H. Davis, Ph.D.,
    Director
Educational Development
    Program

Michigan State University
17 Morrill Hall
East Lansing, MI 48824
(517) 332-6855

Frederick H. Gaige, Ph.D.,
    Dean
Fairleigh Dickinson University
College of Arts and Sciences
Madison, NJ 07940
(201) 377-4700, ext. 339

Tony Grasha, Ph.D.
Associate Professor of
    Psychology
University of Cincinnati
Department of Psychology
McMickon Hall
Cincinnati, OH 45208
(513) 475-2288
(513) 475-3631

Robert S. Jackson, Ph.D.
President and Founder
Robert Jackson and Associates
845 Chicago Avenue
Evanston, IL 60202
(312) 475-1166

Sam H. Lane, Ph.D.
Senior Associate
Projects for Educational
    Development
1836 Euclid Avenue, No. 203
Cleveland, OH 44115

Ronald Lippitt, Ph.D.
President, Human Resource
  Development Associates
Professor Emeritus, Sociology
  and Psychology, U. of
  Michigan
1916 Cambridge Road
Ann Arbor, MI 48104
(313) 663-4740
(313) 994-4616

Charles A. McKee, Ed.D.
Cranbrook Learning Associates
1094 Haslett Road
Haslett, MI 48840

Joan North, Ph.D., Director
Professional Development
Small Colleges Consortium
2000 P Street, NW, No. 400
Washington, DC 20036
(202) 223-6080

Glenn F. Nyre, Ph.D.
Vice President and Executive
  Director
Evaluation and Training
  Institute
12401 Wilshire Boulevard
Suite 304
Los Angeles, CA 90025
(213) 820-8521

Steven R. Phillips, Ph.D.
Director
Associated Schools of the
  Pacific Northwest
University of Puget Sound
1500 North Warner
Tacoma, WA 98407
(206) 756-3340

Gary H. Quehl, Ph.D.,
  President
Council for the Advancement
  of Small Colleges
One Dupont Circle, NW
Washington, DC 20036
(212) 659-3795

Sheryl Riechmann, Ph.D.
University of Massachusetts-
  Amherst
HS/ABS
477 Hills South
Amherst, MA 01003
(413) 545-0868

Clare Rose, Ph.D., President
Evaluation and Training
  Institute
12401 Wilshire Boulevard
Suite 304
Los Angeles, CA 90025
(213) 820-8521

Stephen Scholl, Ph.D., Dean
Educational Services
Academic Affairs Office U-107
Ohio Wesleyan University
Delaware, OH 43015
(614) 369-4431, ext. 710

Stephen L. Yelon, Ph.D.
Professor and Assistant
  Director
Michigan State University
17 Morrill Hall
East Lansing, MI 48824
(517) 353-8942

Carol Zion, Ph.D., Director
Management and Organization
  Development

Miami-Dade Community
College
11380 Northwest 27th Avenue
Miami, FL 33167
(305) 685-4514

B. Medical Education

John Aluise, M.B.A.
Director of Organization and
Development
Department of Family
Medicine
School of Medicine
University of North Carolina
Chapel Hill, NC 27514
(919) 966-4003

Robert Beran, Ph.D.
Associate Director
Association of American
Medical Colleges
One Dupont Circle
Washington, DC 20036
(202) 466-5100

T. Earle Bowen, Jr., Ph.D.
Assistant Vice Chancellor for
Academic Affairs
University of Tennessee Center
Health Sciences
800 Madison Avenue
Memphis, TN 38163
(901) 528-5578

Sam Brown, Ed.D., Director
Office of Educational
Development
University of Alabama
School of Medicine
Box 332, NBSB, University
Station
Birmingham, AL 35294

(205) 943-3053

Charles W. Dohner, Ph.D.
Associate Professor
Office of Research in Medical
Education
University of Washington
School of Medicine
E-312 Health Sciences Building
SC-45
Seattle, WA 98195
(206) 543-2259

James Erdmann, Ph.D.,
Director
Division of Educational
Measurement and Research
Association of American
Medical Colleges
One Dupont Circle
Washington, DC 20036
(202) 466-5166

Hilliard Jason, M.D., Ed. D.
Director
National Center for Faculty
Development
School of Medicine
University of Miami
P.O. Box 016960
Miami, FL 33101
(305) 661-7340

Paul J. Munson, Ed.D.,
Professor
Educational Planning and
Development Program
Medical College of Virginia
Campus
Virginia Commonwealth
University
MCV Station Box 124

Richmond, VA 23298
(804) 786-9779

Ruth Scheuer, M.P.H.
Director of Program Evaluation
Sophie Davis School for
  Biomedical Education
The City College of New York
138th and Convent Avenue
Room 910J
New York, NY 10031
(212) 690-8255-6-7

Gregory L. Trzebiatowski,
  Ph.D.
Associate Dean for Medical
  and Graduate Education
Ohio State University College
  of Medicine
254 Medical Administration
  Center
370 West 9th Avenue
Columbus, OH 43210
(614) 422-6437

SIMULATION

A. Higher Education

Christine McGuire, M.A.
Associate Director
Center for Educational
  Development
University of Illinois
808 South Wood Street
Chicago, IL 60612
(312) 996-3590

Eric Zemper, M.S.
Consultant
Learning and Evaluation
  Service
Michigan State University
202 South Kedzie
East Lansing, MI 48824
(517) 355-3408

B. Medical Education

Stephen Abrahamson, M.D.
Director
Division of Research in Medical
  Education
University of Southern

California
School of Medicine
2025 Zonal Avenue
Los Angeles, CA 90033
(213) 225-2038

Philip Bashook, Ed.D.
Associate Director
Educational Development Unit
Michael Reese School of Health
  Science
530 East 31st
Chicago, IL 60616
(312) 791-5530

Gordon Page, Ed.D., Director
Division of Educational
  Support and Development
Office of the Coordinator of
  Health Sciences
University of British Columbia
Vancouver, British Columbia
Canada V6T 1W5
(604) 228-6641

TEACHING METHODS

A. Higher Education

William Bergquist, Ph.D.
Consultant
1217 Campus Drive
Berkeley, CA 94708
(415) 845-2299

John Centra, Ph.D.
Senior Research Psychologist
Educational Testing Service
Rosedale Road
Princeton, NJ 08540
(609) 921-9000

Robert M. Diamond, Ph.D.
Assistant Vice Chancellor
Center for Instructional
  Development
Syracuse University
115 College Place
Syracuse, NY 13210
(315) 423-4571

Paul L. Dressel, Ph.D.
Professor of University
  Research
Michigan State University
Room 331
Hannah Administration
  Building
East Lansing, MI 48824
(517) 355-6629

John Fry, Ph.D.
Consultant
Learning and Evaluation
  Service
Michigan State University
17 Morrill Hall
East Lansing, MI 48824

(517) 353-4643

Barbara Helling, Ph.D.
Associate Professor of Sociology
Coordinator,
  Teaching/Learning Center
St. Olaf College
Northfield, MN 55057
(507) 663-3139
(507) 663-3247

Sheryl Riechmann, Ph.D.
University of
  Massachusetts — Amherst
HS/ABS
477 Hills South
Amherst, MA 01003
(413) 545-0868

Stephen Scholl, Ph.D., Dean
Educational Services
Academic Affairs Office U-107
Ohio Wesleyan University
Delaware, OH 43015
(614) 369-4431, ext. 710

Luann Wilkerson, Ed.D.
Director, Center for
  Enhancement of Teaching
  Effectiveness
Murray State University
Lowry Center
Murray, KY 42071
(502) 762-2535

Stephen L. Yelon, Ph.D.
Professor and Assistant
  Director
Michigan State University
17 Morrill Hall
East Lansing, MI 48824
(517) 353-8942

B. Medical Education

Stephen Abrahamson, M.D.
Director
Division of Research in Medical
  Education
University of Southern
  California
School of Medicine
2025 Zonal Avenue
Los Angeles, CA 90033
(213) 225-2038

T. Earle Bowen, Jr., Ph.D.
Assistant Vice Chancellor for
  Academic Affairs
University of Tennessee Center
  Health Sciences
800 Madison Avenue
Memphis, TN 38163
(901) 528-5578

Susan A. Brock, Ph.D.
Coordinator of Faculty
  Development
St. Mary's Junior College
2500 South 6th Street
Minneapolis, MN 55454
(612) 332-5521

D. Joseph Clark, Ph.D.,
  Director
Biological Sciences Learning
  Resource Center
University of Washington
Johnson Annex A AK-15
Seattle, WA 98195
(206) 543-6588

Merrel D. Flair, Ph.D.,
  Director
Office of Medical Studies

Professor, Department of
  Psychiatry,
School of Medicine
Clinical Professor, School of
  Education
University of North Carolina
School of Medicine
Chapel Hill, NC 27514
(919) 966-4461

Ed Glassman, Ph.D.
Professor of Biochemistry
University of North Carolina
School of Medicine
Chapel Hill, NC 27514
(919) 966-3163

Robert J. Massad, M.D.
Chairman
Department of Family
  Medicine
Montefiore Hospital
111 East 210th Street
Bronx, NY 10467
(212) 920-5521

Michael Melnick, Ed.D.
Assistant Director for
  Educational Programs
Center for Educational
  Development
University of Illinois
Medical Center Campus
808 South Wood Street—
  Room 986 DMP
Chicago, IL 60612
(312) 996-3590

Bruce Strem, Ph.D., Director
Research in Dental Education
Georgetown University

School of Dentistry
Washington, DC 20007

(202) 625-7283

WORKSHOPS

A. Higher Education

William Bergquist, Ph.D.
Consultant
1217 Campus Drive
Berkeley, CA 94708
(415) 845-2299

Steven R. Phillips, Ph.D.
Director
Associated Schools of the
    Pacific Northwest
University of Puget Sound
1500 North Warner
Tacoma, WA 98407
(206) 756-3340

Eva Schindler-Rainman, Ph.D.
Organizational Consultant
4267 San Rafael Avenue
Los Angeles, CA 90042
(213) 257-8962

B. Medical Education

Carole Bland, Ph.D.
Associate Professor
Department of Family Practice

and Community Health
University of Minnesota
Medical School
Box 381 Mayo
516 Delaware Street, SE
Minneapolis, MN 55455
(612) 376-3689
(612) 376-3317

Sandra Inglis, Ed.D., Director
Educational Development and
    Resources
College of Osteopathic
    Medicine
Ohio University
Athens, OH 45701
(614) 594-6401, ext. 275

Robert J. Massad, M.D.
Chairman
Department of Family
    Medicine
Montefiore Hospital
111 East 210th Street
Bronx, NY 10467
(212) 920-5521

OTHER SPECIALTIES

A. Higher Education

Bert R. Biles, M.D.
Special Assistant for Sponsored
    Programs
The Graduate School
Fairchild Hall
Kansas State University
Manhattan, KS 66506
(913) 532-6194

Area of Specialty:
    Grantsmanship; health care
    delivery

Frederick H. Gaige, Ph.D.
Dean
College of Arts and Sciences
Fairleigh Dickinson University
Madison, NJ 07940
(201) 377-4700, ext. 339

Area of Specialty:
Administrative development;
Dean's role in faculty
development

Donald P. Hoyt, Ph.D.
Assistant Vice-President for
Academic Affairs
Kansas State University
Manhattan, KS 66506
(913) 532-5712
Area of Specialty:
Measurement; political
dynamics; relating evaluation
to development

Ronald Lippitt, Ph.D.
President
Human Resource Development
Associates
1916 Cambridge Road
Ann Arbor, MI 48104
(313) 994-4616
Area of Specialty: Creating
change; long-range
planning, interorganization
collaboration; teambuilding;
management development

Joan North, Ph.D.
Director, Professional
Development
Small Colleges Consortium
2000 P Street, NW
Suite 400
Washington, DC 20036
(203) 223-6080
Area of Specialty:
Administrative development;
personal/professional growth
plans

B. Medical Education

John Aluise, M.B.A.
Director of Organization and
Development
Department of Family
Medicine
School of Medicine
University of North Carolina
Chapel Hill, NC 27514
(919) 966-4003
Area of Specialty: Management
education

Sam Brown, Ed.D.
Director
Office of Educational
Development
School of Medicine
University of Alabama
Box 332, NBSB, University
Station
Birmingham, AL 35294
(205) 943-3053
Area of Specialty:
Administrative management

Wayne K. Davis, Ph.D.
Director, Office of Educational
Resources and Research
University of Michigan
G 1111 Towsley Center
Ann Arbor, MI 48109
(313) 763-1153
Area of Specialty: Educational
psychology applied to health
science education

J. J. Guilbert, M.D., Ph.D.
Chief, Educational Planning
Division of Health Manpower
Development

World Health Organization
1211 Geneva 27,
  SWITZERLAND
Geneva: 346061, ext. 2505
Area of Specialty: Faculty
  development; curriculum
  design

Ilene Harris, M.A.
Research Associate
University of Minnesota
  Medical School Curriculum
  Affairs
Box 33 Mayo
420 Delaware Street, SE
Minneapolis, MN 55455
(612) 376-7241
Area of Specialty: Educational
  research and evaluation

Tom Held, Ed.D.
Director of Media
University of Maryland
School of Medicine
Baltimore, MD 21201
(301) 528-6975
Area of Specialty: Computer-
  based education; script
  writing for medical television

Libby Hruska, Ed.D.
Teaching Consultant
303 Homestead Avenue
Holyoke, MA 01040
(413) 534-7000
Area of Specialty: Teaching
  improvement; workshops on
  communication, life-
  planning, stress
  management, time
  management, goal setting

Hilliard Jason, M.D., Ed.D.
Director
National Center for Faculty
  Development
School of Medicine
University of Miami
P.O. Box 016960
Miami, FL 33101
(305) 661-7340
Area of Specialty: Humanizing
  the educational process;
  facilitating personal and
  institutional change

Henry C. Johnson, Ph.D.
Director
Office of Research and
  Development in Medical
  Education
CMDNJ-Rutgers Medical
  School
P.O. Box 101, University
  Heights
Piscataway, NJ 08854
Area of Specialty: Evaluation;
  instructional planning;
  faculty development

Norman Kagan, Ph.D.
Professor
College of Education
Michigan State University
East Lansing, MI 48823
(517) 355-3271
Area of Specialty:
  Interpersonal communication
  between faculty and
  students, and between
  students and patients;
  doctor-patient relations;

. patient education; counseling

W. Robert Kennedy, Ph.D.
Director
Division of Research in Medical
  Education
School of Medicine
Case Western Reserve
  University
2119 Abington Road
Cleveland, OH 44106
(216) 368-3448
Area of Specialty: Educational
  psychology; CME
  administration

Stephen P. Mihalich, D.O.
Assistant Clinical Professor,
  MSU/COM
5075 Midmoor Road
Bloomfield Hills, MI 48013
(313) 626-7725
Area of Specialty: Clinical
  osteopathic medical
  education; postdoctoral

continuing medical
education; medical
administration

Victor Neufeld, M.D.
Director, Program for
  Educational Development
Faculty of McMaster University
1200 Main Street, West
Hamilton, Ontario
CANADA
(416) 525-9140 (2113)
Area of Specialty: Clinical
  problem solving

Thomas F. Santucci, Jr., D.O.
Professor and Chairman
Department of Pediatrics
New Jersey School of
  Osteopathic Medicine
Camden, NJ 08103
(609) 757-2646
Area of Specialty: Case
  presentations; continuing
  medical education; residency

REFERENCES

1. Milton, Shoben, quoted by Gaff JC: *Toward Faculty Renewal: Advances in Faculty, Instructional and Organizational Development.* San Francisco, Jossey-Bass, 1975.
2. Francis JB: How do we get there from here? Program design for faculty development. *Journal of Higher Education* 46:719-732, November/December 1975.
3. Gaff JC: *Toward Faculty Renewal: Advances in Faculty, Instructional and Organizational Development.* San Francisco, Jossey-Bass, 1975.
4. Rogers EM, Shoemaker F: *Communication of Innovations.* New York, Free Press, 1971.
5. Bland CJ: Guidelines for planning faculty development workshops. *Journal of Family Practice* 5:235-241, August 1977.
6. Centra JA: Faculty development practices. *New Directions for Higher Education* 17:49-55, Spring 1977.
7. Wergin JF, Mason EJ, Munson PJ: The practice of faculty development: An experience-derived model. *Journal of Higher Education* 47:289-308, May/June 1976.
8. Donnelly FA, Ware JE, Wolkon GH, et al: Evaluation of weekend seminars for physicians. *Journal of Medical Education* 47:184-187, March 1972.
9. Nerup J, Thomson O, Vejlsgaard R: Teaching the teacher to teach: Results of three experiments. *Danish Medical Bulletin* 19:198-201, September 1972.
10. Koen FM: A faculty educational development program and an evaluation of its evaluation. *Journal of Medical Education* 51:854-855, October 1976.
11. Society of Teachers of Family Medicine: *A Pilot Program of Training Workshops for Faculty in Family Practice Medicine: Final Report* (Contract No. HRA-231-76-0018). Washington, DC, US Department of Health, Education, and Welfare, Health Resources Administration, 1977.
12. Reineke RA, Welch WW: Workshops for Faculty Development in Family Medicine. Unpublished consultants' report to the Society of Teachers of Family Medicine, 1977.
13. Reineke RA, Bland CJ: Follow-up Evaluation Report for Workshops for Faculty Development in Family Medicine. Unpublished consultants' report to the Society of Teachers of Family Medicine, 1978.
14. Bland CJ, Reineke RA, Welch WW, Shahady EJ: Effectiveness of faculty development workshops in family medicine. *Journal of Family Practice* 9:453-458, September 1979.
15. Adams, ER, Ham TH, Mawardi BH, et al: Research in self-education for clinical teachers. *Journal of Medical Education* 49:1166-1173, December 1974.
16. Bergquist WH, Phillips SR: *A Handbook for Faculty Development.*

Washington, DC, Council for the Advancement of Small Colleges and College Center of the Finger Lakes, 1975.

17. Guilbert JJ: *How To Organize a Short Educational Workshop.* Geneva, World Health Organization, 1976.

18. Will E, Casbergue J (eds): *Workshop Planning: A Guide to Considering, Designing and Planning Educational Workshops.* East Lansing, Michigan State University, Office of Medical Educational Research and Development, 1976.

19. 50 Steps to a Successful Meeting. Poster by Bureau of Business and Technology Inc, New York, 1976.

20. Bergquist WH, Phillips SR: Components of an effective faculty development program. *Journal of Higher Education* 46:177-211, March/April 1975.

21. Connell KJ: Organizing short-term teacher-training programmes. In Center for Education Development, Illinois School of Medicine (ed): *Development of Educational Programmes for the Health Professions.* Geneva, World Health Organization, 1973, pp. 93-103.

22. Gregory ID, Hammar B: Case study of first course in teaching skills and methods for university medical staff. *British Journal of Medical Education* 8:92-98, June 1974.

23. Gale J, Anderson J, Freeling P, et al: Planning of educational courses — A model of the management of an educational workshop for teachers of medicine. *British Journal of Medical Education* 8:87-91, June 1974.

24. World Health Organization: *Training and Preparation of Teachers for Schools of Medicine and Allied Health Sciences* (Technical Report Series No. 521). Geneva, World Health Organization, 1973.

25. Wergin JF: So you want to try faculty development? Paper presented at the annual meeting of the American Educational Research Association, Washington, DC, 1975.

26. Anderson SB, Ball S, Murphy RT, et al: *Encyclopedia of Educational Evaluation: Concepts and Techniques for Evaluating Education and Training.* San Francisco, Jossey-Bass, 1973.

27. Phillips SR: The many faces of faculty development. *College Management* 9:14, 17, November/December 1974.

28. Centra JA: *Strategies for Improving College Teaching* (Report 8). Washington, DC, US Department of Health, Education, and Welfare, Office of Education, 1972. (ERIC Document Reproduction Service No. ED 071 616).

29. Davis LN, McCallon E: *Planning, Conducting, and Evaluating Workshops: A Practitioner's Guide to Adult Education.* Austin, Tex, Learning Concepts, 1974.

30. Quehl GH, quoted by Gaff JC: *Toward Faculty Renewal: Advances in Faculty, Instructional and Organizational Development.* San Francisco, Jossey-Bass, 1976.

31. Fulop T: Training teachers of health personnel. In Center for Educational Development, Illinois College of Medicine (ed): *Development of Educational Programmes for the Health Professions.* Geneva, World

Health Organization, 1973, pp 84-92.

32. Connell KJ, Alberti JM, Piotrowski ZH: What does it take for faculty development to make a difference? *Educational Horizons* 55:108-115, Winter 1976-77.

33. Johnson K: Strategies for Building Successful Community-Based Family Practice Residency Programs. Unpublished workshop coordinator's report to the Society of Teachers of Family Medicine, 1977.

34. Jason H, Slotnick HB, Lefever RD, et al: *Faculty Development Survey Final Report.* Washington, DC, American Association of Medical Colleges, Division of Faculty Development, December 1977.

35. *Catalog of Federal Domestic Assistance.* Washington, DC, US Government Printing Office, 1978.

36. Lewis MO (ed): *Foundation Directory,* ed 6. Irvington, NY, Columbia University Press, 1977.

37. *Annual Register of Grant Support, 1978-1979,* ed 5. Chicago, Marquis Academic Media, 1978.

38. Capriotti BJ, Capriotti FJ III: *Minnesota Foundation Directory.* Minneapolis, Foundation Data Center, 1977.

39. Capriotti BJ, Capriotti FJ III: *Illinois Foundation Directory.* Minneapolis, Foundation Data Center, 1978.

40. *Foundation Grants Index, 1978.* Irvington, NY, Columbia University Press, 1978.

41. White VP: *Grants: How to Find Out About Them and What to Do Next.* New York, Plenum Press, 1975.

42. Kiritz NJ: Program planning and proposal writing. *Grantsmanship Center News* 3:11-14, January 1974.

43. Guilbert JJ: *Educational Handbook.* Geneva, World Health Organization, 1976.

44. Mager RF: *Preparing Instructional Objectives,* ed 2. Belmont, Calif, Fearon, 1975.

45. Arsham GM, Good N: Determination of internship objectives. *Journal of Medical Education* 49:446-448, May 1974.

46. Bacchus H: Preparing educational objectives in internal medicine. *Journal of Medical Education* 47:708-711, September 1972.

47. Baker EL, Popham WJ: *Expanding Dimensions of Instructional Objectives.* Englewood Cliffs, NJ, Prentice-Hall, 1973.

48. *Educational Objectives for Certification in Family Medicine.* Toronto, College of Family Physicians of Canada, 1974.

49. Cassata DM, Harris IB, Bland CJ, et al: A systematic approach to curriculum design in a medical school interview course. *Journal of Medical Education* 51:939-942, November 1976.

50. DePalma RG, Izant RJ, Jordan A, et al: Objectives and methods in undergraduate surgical education. *Surgery* 75:915-924, June 1974.

51. Duchastel PC, Merrill PF: The effects of behavioral objectives on learning: A review of empirical studies. *Review of Educational Research* 43:53-69, Winter 1973.

52. Eisner EW: Educational objectives: Help or hindrance? *School Review* 75:250-266, Autumn 1967.

53. Glaser R: Instructional technology and the measurement of learning outcomes: Some questions. *American Psychologist* 18:519-521, August 1963.

54. Miles DT, Kibler RJ, Pettigrew LE: The effects of study questions on college students' test performance. *Psychology in the Schools* 4:25-26, January 1967.

55. Morreau LE: Behavioral objectives: Analysis and application. In Maloney HB (ed): *Accountability and the Teaching of English.* Urbana, Ill, National Council of Teachers of English, 1972.

56. Salkin LM, Hildebrand CN, Landay MA: Behavioral objectives — A review of the problems. *Journal of Dental Education* 38:399-402, July 1974.

57. Schuck RF, Watson CG, Shapiro AP, et al: The use of behavioral objectives in the development and evaluation of a third-year surgical clerkship. *Journal of Medical Education* 49:604-607, June 1974.

58. Spivey BE: Developing objectives in ophthalmologic education. *American Journal of Ophthalmology* 68:439-445, September 1969.

59. Stritter FT, Bowles LT: The teacher as manager: A strategy for medical education. *Journal of Medical Education* 47:93-101, February 1972.

60. Varagunam T: Student awareness of behavioral objectives: The effect on learning. *British Journal of Medical Education* 5:213-216, September 1971.

61. Palinchak RS: Behavioral objectives: To be or not to be. *Improving College and University Teaching* 23:155-156, Summer 1975.

62. Rovin S, Packer MW: Evaluation of teaching and teachers at the University of Kentucky College of Dentistry: I. Development and evaluation criteria. *Journal of Dental Education* 35:496-501, August 1971.

63. Popham WJ, Baker EL: *Establishing Instructional Goals.* Englewood Cliffs, NJ, Prentice-Hall, 1970.

64. Gronlund NE: *Stating Behavioral Objectives for Classroom Instruction.* New York, MacMillan, 1970.

65. Hannah LS, Michaelis JV: *A Comprehensive Framework for Educational Objectives: A Guide to Systematic Planning and Evaluation.* Reading, Mass, Addison-Wesley, 1977.

66. Bland CJ, Houge DR, Hofstrand HJ, et al: Developing an objective based curriculum for a family practice residency, *Journal of Family Practice* 4:103-110, January 1977.

67. Mager RF: *Goal Analysis.* Belmont, Calif, Fearon, 1972.

68. Cantrell T: How do medical-school staff learn to teach? *Lancet* 2:724-747, September 29, 1973.

69. Peck RJ, Tucker JA: Research on teacher education. In Travers RMW (ed): *Second Handbook of Research on Teaching.* Chicago, Rand-McNally, 1973.

70. Fisch AL: The trigger film technique. *Improving College and University Teaching* 20:286-289, Autumn 1972.

71. Travers RMW (ed): *Second Handbook of Research on Teaching.* Chicago, Rand-McNally, 1973.

72. Slotnick HB: *Taxonomy of Teaching Practices.* Staff report for the Association of American Medical Colleges, Division of Faculty Development, December 1975.

73. Allen D, Ryan K: *Microteaching.* Reading, Mass, Addison-Wesley, 1969.

74. Emmer ET, Millett GB: *An Assessment of Terminal Performance in a Teaching Laboratory: A Pilot Study.* Austin, Tex, University of Texas Research and Development Center for Teacher Education, August 1968. (ERIC Document Reproduction Service No. ED 055 981).

75. Prentice ED, Metcalf WK: A teaching workshop for medical educators. *Journal of Medical Education* 49:1031-1034, November 1974.

76. Perlberg A, Peri JN, Weinreb M, et al: Microteaching and videotape recordings: A new approach to improving teaching. *Journal of Medical Education* 47:43-50, January 1972.

77. Millett GB: *Comparison of Training Procedures for Promoting Teacher and Learner Translation Behavior* (Technical Report No. 9). Stanford, Calif, Stanford University Center for Research and Development in Teaching, 1969. (ERIC Document Reproduction Service No. ED 035 600).

78. Wedberg DP, Finn JD: *A Comparative Investigation of the Instructional and Administrative Efficiency of Various Observational Techniques in the Introductory Course in Education.* Los Angeles, University of Southern California, 1963.

79. Steinen RF: An exploratory study of the results of providing increased feedback to student teachers of mathematics (Doctoral dissertation, Ohio State University, 1967). *Dissertation Abstracts International,* 1966, *27,* 2929A. (University Microfilms No. 67-2544).

80. Human Development in Higher Education Group: *Faculty Development in a Time of Retrenchment.* New Rochelle, NY, Change Magazine Press, 1974.

81. Holcomb JD, Garner AE: *Improving Teaching in Medical Schools: A Practical Handbook.* Springfield, Ill, Thomas, 1973.

82. Gordon MJ: Research traditions available to family medicine. *Journal of Family Practice* 7:59-68, July 1978.

83. Ford CW, Morgan MK: *Teaching in the Health Professions.* St. Louis, Mosby, 1976.

84. Ford CW: *Clinical Education for the Allied Health Professions.* St. Louis, Mosby, 1978.

85. Morgan MK, Irby DM: *Evaluating Clinical Competence in the Health Professions.* St. Louis, Mosby, 1978.

86. Miller GE (ed), Abrahamson SA, Cohen IS, et al: *Teaching and Learning in Medical School.* Cambridge, Mass, Harvard University Press, 1961.

87. Gaff SS, Festa C, Gaff JG: *Professional Development: A Guide to Resources.* New Rochelle, NY, Change Magazine Press, 1979.

88. Morris LL, Fitz-Gibbon CT: *Evaluator's Handbook.* Beverly Hills, Calif, Sage, 1978.

89. Morris LL, Fitz-Gibbon CT: *How to Deal With Goals and Objectives.* Beverly

Hills, Calif, Sage, 1978.

90. Fitz-Gibbon CT, Morris LL: *How to Design a Program Evaluation.* Beverly Hills, Calif, Sage, 1978.

91. Morris LL, Fitz-Gibbon CT: *How to Measure Program Implementation.* Beverly Hills, Calif, Sage, 1978.

92. Henerson ME, Morris LL, Fitz-Gibbon CT: *How to Measure Attitudes.* Beverly Hills, Calif, Sage, 1978.

93. Morris LL, Fitz-Gibbon CT: *How to Measure Achievement.* Beverly Hills, Calif, Sage, 1978.

94. Fitz-Gibbon CT, Morris LL: *How to Calculate Statistics.* Beverly Hills, Calif, Sage, 1978.

95. Morris LL, Fitz-Gibbon CT: *How to Present an Evaluation Report.* Beverly Hills, Calif, Sage, 1978.

96. Howard GS, Daily PR: Response-shift bias: A source of contamination of self-report measures. *Journal of Applied Psychology* 64:144-150, April 1979.

97. Howard GS, Ralph KM, Gulanick NA, et al: Internal invalidity in pretest-posttest self-report evaluations and a reevaluation of retrospective pretests. *Applied Psychological Measurement* 3:1-23, Winter 1979.

98. Howard GS, Schmeck RR, Bray JH: Internal invalidity in studies employing self-report instruments: A suggested remedy. *Journal of Educational Measurement* 16:129-135, Summer 1979.

99. Worthen BR, Sanders JR: *Educational Evaluation: Theory and Practice.* Belmont, Calif, CA Jones, 1973.

100. Struening E: *Handbook of Evaluation Research.* Beverly Hills, Calif, Sage, 1975, vol. 1.

101. Guttentag NG: *Handbook of Evaluation Research.* Beverly Hills, Calif, Sage, 1975, vol 2.

BIBLIOGRAPHY

AAFP teacher resource registry lists 700 practicing physicians. *AAFP Reporter* 3:5, October 1976.

Adams W, Banham GW, Bowen H, et al: *Colleges and Money: A Faculty Guide to Academic Economics.* New Rochelle, NY, Change Magazine Press, 1976.

American Association of Junior Colleges, Faculty Development Project. *In-service Training for Two-year College Faculty and Staff: A Survey of Junior and Community College Administrators.* Washington DC, Author, 1969. (ERIC Document Reproduction Service No. ED 034 519).

Anderson, J, Day JL, Freeling P, et al: The workshop as a learning system in medical teacher education. *British Journal of Medical Education* 6:296-300, 1972.

Arsham GM: An instructional skills workshop for medical teachers: Design and execution. *British Journal of Medical Education* 5:320-324, December 1971.

Barrows HS, Tamblyn RM, Jenkins M: Preparing faculty for innovative educational roles. *Journal of Medical Education* 51:592-594, July 1976.

Bayley DH: Making college teaching a profession. *Improving College and University Teaching* 15:115-119, Spring 1967.

Bevan JM: Faculty development (A votre sante). Paper prepared for Workshop for New Academic Deans, Association of American Colleges, and Council of Colleges of Arts and Sciences, Estes Park, Col, June 23-28, 1974.

Birnbaum R: Using the calendar for faculty development. *Educational Record* 56:226-230, Fall 1975.

Bland CJ: Partial summary of questionnaire on continuing education in faculty development. Paper prepared for the Society of Teachers of Family Medicine, Kansas City, Mo, September 1976.

Borg WR: The mini-course as a vehicle for changing teacher behavior: The research evidence. Paper presented at the annual meeting of the American Educational Research Association, Los Angeles, Calif, February 1969.

Bowdler AJ, Wallace N: The role of overseas experiences in the education of the medical student. *Journal of Medical Education* 49:1035-1039, November 1974.

Bradley AP Jr: A role for faculty in contract learning: Toward a theory of nontraditional faculty development. Paper presented at the National Conference on Higher Education, March 1975. (ERIC Document Reproduction Service No. ED 111 307).

Center for Educational Development, Illinois College of Medicine (ed): *Development of Educational Programmes for the Health Professions.* Geneva, World Health Organization, 1973.

Chickering AW: *Experience and Learning: An Introduction to Experiential Learning.* New Rochelle, NY, Change Magazine Press, 1977.

Claxton CS: Comprehensive staff development program: Implications for the office of instructional research and planning. *Faculty Development and Evaluation in Higher Education* 2:6-14, Winter 1977.

Clements CC Jr: *How Staff Development Works in the Small Community College.* Lake City, Fla, Lake City Community College, 1973. (ERIC Document Reproduction Service No. ED 093 398).

Community College Faculty Development. Brief prepared for the American Association of Community and Junior Colleges 1973 Assembly. Warrenton, Va, November 29-December 1, 1973. (ERIC Document Reproduction Service No. ED 081 411).

Costin F: A graduate course in the teaching of psychology: Description and evaluation. *Journal of Teacher Education* 19:425-432, Winter 1968.

Cotsonas NJ Jr, Kaiser HF: Student evaluation of clinical teaching. *Journal of Medical Education* 39:742-745, September 1963.

Cox R, Kontiainen S: Comparison of attitudes of trained trainers, untrained trainers, and trainees to teaching in general practice. *British Journal of Medical Education* 8:103-110, June 1974.

Cross KP: Not can, but will college teaching be improved? *New Directions for Higher Education* 17:1-15, Spring 1977.

Davis S, Gross-Davis B: Assessing teacher effectiveness based on student learning gains. *California Journal of Educational Research* 25:186-191, September 1974.

Eble KE: *Career Development of the Effective College Teacher.* American Association of University Professors, Washington DC: Association of American Colleges, Washington DC, November 1971. (ERIC Document Reproduction Service No. ED 089 630).

Eden H: *Faculty Development and Evaluation: Annotated Bibliography and Other References.* Washington DC, Association of American Medical Colleges, Division of Faculty Development, 1975.

The Evaluation of Community College Teaching: Models in Theory and Practice. Proceedings of Evaluation of Teaching Conference sponsored by the California Junior College Association, Burlingame, Calif, April 13, 1972. (ERIC Document Reproduction Service No. ED 063 923).

Expert Committee on Professional and Technical Education of Medical and Auxiliary Personnel (Technical Report Series No. 69). Geneva, World Health Organization, 1953.

Fink LD: Developing temporary faculty: The challenge posed by teaching assistants. *Education Horizons* 55:56-63, Winter 1976-77.

Freedman M: Facilitating faculty development. *New Directions for Higher Education* 1:105-111, Spring 1973.

Freedman M, Sanford N: The faculty member yesterday and today. *New Directions for Higher Education* 1:1-16, Spring 1973.

Gaff JG, Armour RS, Foster VB, et al: Project on institutional renewal through the improvement of teaching. *Educational Horizons* 55:97-103, Winter 1976-77.

Gerth DR: Institutional approaches to faculty development. *New Directions for Higher Education* 1:83-92, Spring 1973.

Gleazer EJ JR: Preparation of junior college teachers. *Educational Record* 48:147-

152, Spring 1967.

Grasha AF: *Assessing and Developing Faculty Performance: Principles and Models.* Cincinnati, Communication and Education Associates, 1977.

Gray CE: The teaching model and evaluation of teaching performance. *Journal of Higher Education* 40:636-642, November 1969.

Gross R: Faculty growth contracts. *Educational Horizons* 55:74-79, Winter 1976-77.

Gustafson KL: Improving instructional development: Faculty as learners. *Educational Technology* 15:34-38, May 1975.

Halliburton D: *How To Succeed as a New Teacher.* New Rochelle, NY, Change Magazine Press, 1978.

Hammons JO: Suggestions concerning institutional training of new faculty. *Community College Review* 1:49-60, July/August 1973.

Hammons JO, Smith Wallace TH: Sixteen ways to kill a college faculty development program. *Educational Technology* 16:16-20, December 1976.

Helfer RE: Peer evaluation: Its potential usefulness in medical education. *British Journal of Medical Education* 6:224-231, September 1972.

Higley H, Hanavan F, King E, et al: *Manual for Allied Health Faculty Development in Short Term Educational Programs* (DHEW Publication No. (HRA) 77-36). Washington DC, US Department of Health, Education, and Welfare, Bureau of Health Manpower, May 1977.

Hildebrand M: The character and skills of the effective professor. *Journal of Higher Education* 44:41-50, January 1973.

Hofstrand H: *The Minnesota Experience.* Manual prepared for the faculty and residents of the Department of Family Practice and Community Health, University of Minnesota, 1977.

Holcomb JD, Garner AE: *Improving Teaching in Medical Schools: A Practical Handbook.* Springfield, Thomas, 1973.

Jason H: An association program for medical faculty development. *Educational Horizons* 55:70-73, Winter 1976-77.

Jason H: Effective medical teachers: Born or made? *Journal of Medical Education* 38:46-47, January 1963.

Kapfer MB, Della-Piana GM: Educational technology in the inservice education of university teaching fellows. *Educational Technology* 14:22-28, July 1974.

Koen F: The training of graduate student teaching assistants. *Educational Record* 49:92-102, Winter 1968.

Lee CBT (ed): *Improving College Teaching.* Washington DC: American Council on Education, 1967.

Linden G: Multi-institutional, multi-level faculty development program. *Educational Horizons* 55:64-69, Winter 1976-77.

Lindquist JD: Self-renewal: Dusting off a new cliche. In Werkama GR (ed): *Faculty Development Project Resource Notebook.* Washington DC, Council for the Advancement of Small Colleges, 1974.

Mackenzie RS: Essential features of a faculty evaluation program. *Journal of Dental Education* 41:301-306, June 1977.

Martin WB: Faculty development as human development. *Liberal Education*

61:187-196, May 1975.

McKeachie WJ: Research on teaching at the college and university level. In Gate NL (ed): *Handbook of Research on Teaching.* Chicago, Rand — McNally, 1963.

McKeachie WJ: *Teaching Tips: A Guidebook for the Beginning College Teacher.* Lexington, Mass, DC Heath, 1969.

McKeachie WJ: *Research on College Teaching: A Review* (Report 6). Washington DC, ERIC Clearinghouse on Higher Education, 1970. (ERIC Document Reproduction Service No. ED 043 789).

McKeachie WJ, Kulik JA: Effective college teaching. In Kerlinger FN (ed): *Review of Research in Education,* ed 3. Itasca, Ill., Peacock, 1975.

Menefee S: *Faculty Development in the Junior College.* A second interim report on the Program with Developing Institutions, 1969-1970. American Association of Junior Colleges, Washington DC, Program with Developing Institutions. (ERIC Document Reproduction Service No. ED 052 773).

Miller GE: Educational science and education for medicine. *British Journal of Medical Education* 1:156-159, June 1967.

Milton O, Edgerly JW: *Testing and Grading of Students.* New Rochelle, NY, Change Magazine Press, 1977.

Morris W (ed): *Effective College Teaching: The Quest for Relevance.* Washington DC, American Council on Education, 1970.

Morrissy JR, McWhinney IR, Biehn JT, et al: Faculty development at the department of family medicine, University of Western Ontario. *Canadian Family Physician* 23:80-94, December 1977.

Neff CB: Faculty development tug o'war, or up a tree with a tuning fork. *Liberal Education* 62:427-431, October 1976.

Noonan JF: Curriculum change: A strategy for improving teaching. In Vermilye DW (ed): *The Expanding Campus: Current Issues in Higher Education.* San Francisco, Jossey-Bass, 1972.

O'Connell WR Jr, Meeth LR: *Evaluating Teaching Improvement Programs.* New Rochelle, NY, Change Magazine Press, 1978.

Osterman DN, Purvis BP, Harrison WL: *Improving Undergraduate Teaching Through a Faculty Development Program.* Corvallis, Ore, Oregon State University, April 1976. (ERIC Document Reproduction Service No. ED 122 836).

Pochyly DF: Problem-oriented faculty development in a medical school. *Educational Horizons* 55:92-96, Winter 1976-77.

Ralph N: Stages of faculty development. *New Directions for Higher Education* 1:61-68, Spring 1973.

Reichsman F, Browning FE, Hinshaw JR: Observations of undergraduate clinical teaching in action. *Journal of Medical Education* 39:147-163, February 1964.

Rosenshine B, Furst N: The use of direct observation to study teaching. In Travers RMW (ed): *Second Handbook of Research on Teaching.* Chicago, Rand-McNally, 1973.

Rous SN, Bamford JC, Gromisch D, et al: The improvement of faculty teaching through evaluation: A preliminary report. *Journal of Surgical Research*

11:311-315, June 1971.

Rous SN, Bamford JC Jr, Gromisch D, et al: The improvement of faculty teaching through evaluation: A follow-up report. *Journal of Surgical Research* 13: 262-266, November 1972.

Roush RE, Holcomb DJ: Teaching improvements in higher education: Medical education may be the leader. *Phi Delta Kappan* 65:338-340, January 1974.

Sanford N: Academic culture and the teacher's development. *Soundings* 54:357-371, Winter 1971.

Sikes W, Barrett L: *Case Studies on Faculty Development*, Quehl GH (ed). Washington DC, Council for the Advancement of Small Colleges, November 1976.

Sinatra LJ: Performance based teacher education: It can be transformational. *Educational Technology* 13:60-63, August 1973.

Stice JE: A bargain at any price; a steal @ $1.24. *Educational Horizons* 55:80-85, Winter 1976-77.

Stritter FT, Hain JD, Grimes DA: Clinical teaching reexamined. *Journal of Medical Education* 50:876-882, September 1975.

Strode OB: Can the human dimensions in medical education be reestablished? *Educational Horizons* 55:104-107, Winter 1976-77.

Tamir P: Invitations to inquiry and teacher training. *The American Professional Teacher* 38:50-52, January 1976.

Toombs W: A three-dimensional view of faculty development. *Journal of Higher Education* 46:701-717, November/December 1975.

Webb J, Smith AB: Improving instruction in higher education. *Education Horizons* 55:86-91, Winter 1976-77.

Weinberger HL: An attempt to identify frequency of use of technical skills and procedures by the primary care physician. *The Journal of Pediatrics* 88, Part I:671-675, April 1976.

Whitely ST, Doyle KO: Dimensions of effective teaching: Factors or artifacts. Symposium presented by the Measurement Division at the meeting of the American Educational Research Association, April 1975.

INDEX

R
833.5
. B55

R
833.5
.B55

R
833.5
.B55